Just by Believing

Justification is an act of God whereby he pronounces all who truly believe 'not guilty' of sin and covers them with the all sufficient righteousness of Christ.

Justification by faith

'This is the truth of the gospel. It is also the principal article of all Christian doctrine, wherein the knowledge of all godliness consisteth. Most necessary it is, therefore, that we should know this article well, teach it unto others, and beat it into their heads continually.'

(Martin Luther, *Epistle to the Galatians*, James Clarke, p.101)

Just by Believing

Frank Allred

Grace Publications

GRACE PUBLICATIONS TRUST
7 Arlington Way
London EC1R 1XA
England
e-mail: AGBCSE@aol.com

Managing Editors:
T. I. Curnow
M. J. Adams

© Grace Publications Trust

First published 2008
ISBN 0946462755
ISBN-13 978-0-946462-75-9

Distributed by
EVANGELICAL PRESS
Faverdale North Industrial Estate
Darlington DL3 OPH
England

e-mail: sales@evangelicalpress.org
www.evangelicalpress.org

Printed and bound in Great Britain by
Biddles Ltd, King's Lynn, Norfolk

Contents

To the Reader

How can I be put right with God? No question can be more important than this. It may be posed in different ways. How can God look with favour upon me, a sinner? How can he accept me as a righteous person when I am guilty of breaking his commandments? How can I, a lawbreaker, appear before him as one who is 'not guilty'?

In our postmodern society, many people today would not have the slightest interest in this question. They have persuaded themselves that anything to do with 'God' is irrelevant. If they do not come to a better mind, they will bear the consequences of their folly. Others would insist that we must allow for a variety of answers, all of which will be true for the persons who give them. All I can say to them is that if they persist in this madness, they put themselves beyond hope. Truth is not capricious. Just as God is unchanging, so his truth is unchanging.

Others assume that God will assess our lives by putting the good on one side of the scales and the bad on the other. The result will determine whether or not we are fit to enter heaven. This is a counsel of despair and the product of ignorance. Generally speaking, those who believe this have convinced themselves that their good deeds will outweigh their bad ones. The idea rests on the arrogant assumption that human beings have the ability to please

God and put him in our debt. Just as we earn our wages by doing a good day's work, so we inherit the kingdom of heaven by our own efforts. Church people in particular are easily afflicted with this self-righteous attitude. Some even think of their church attendance as a deposit in their heavenly bank account.

Then we have the Universalists who believe that since God loves everyone, everyone will be saved. Hell does not exist. The huge amount of space in the Bible given over to teaching about divine judgment is conveniently ignored. If you do not like it, then you do not read it.

Those who love and believe the Bible cannot go along with any of this. They no longer see heaven as a reward for their own goodness. They know that the only way in which sinners may be justified before God and reconciled to him, is by faith in Jesus Christ. He is the only one who is able to save us from everlasting destruction. He is the only hope of mankind, for 'Salvation is found in no-one else, for there is no other name under heaven given to men by which we must be saved' (Acts 4:12).

As Paul the apostle puts it, '…a righteousness from God, apart from law, has been made known, to which the Law and the Prophets testify. This righteousness from God comes through faith in Jesus Christ to all who believe' (Rom. 3:21-22). Christ is the holy and righteous one. The repenting and believing sinner is sheltered for ever under Christ's perfect righteousness.

Critics who are familiar with the Scripture teaching on justification but do not believe it, are always ready to find fault. If God justifies us on the basis of faith alone, they say, we would be free to break his commands with impunity. Being good would serve no purpose. The doctrine of justification by faith, if it were true, would be a spur to sin.

Those who argue in this way do not know what they are talking about. All who have the assurance that they are justified by faith are keenly aware of a God-given desire to live holy lives. Moreover, they are quick to repent of their sins. For those who feel the burden of their sins and are aware of its dreadful consequences, nothing spurs them on to holy living like the teaching of the Scriptures on this subject.

To the Church's incalculable loss, the doctrine is now so neglected as to be almost forgotten. Martin Luther rightly regarded it as 'the principal article of all Christian doctrine' (*Epistle to the Galatians*, James Clarke, p.101). Indeed, without justification by faith there is no gospel. To say that the downgrading of the subject is a tragedy would be an understatement. The majority, including many who go regularly to church, are totally ignorant of it.

Many ministers, too, are ignorant. Some know of the doctrine but disapprove of it. Some disagree so strongly with Paul's teaching that they either publicly criticise him, or quietly exclude his teaching from their pulpit ministry. Such ministers are not fulfilling their duty to declare the whole will of God (Acts 20:27), nor are they contending for the faith once entrusted to the saints (Jude 3).

Oddly enough, although it is not commonly known, the doctrine of justification by faith is again the subject of fierce debate in the academic world. I say 'again' because it has long been a cause of division, especially between Roman Catholic and Protestant scholars.

Even between scholars who are pleased to call themselves evangelical, there is little agreement. Some claim to have new perspectives on the way Paul should be understood. After two thousand years, this seems rather conceited to say the least. The teaching of Augustine, Calvin, Luther, Owen and many others is not so easily set aside. We ought to be thankful for those scholars who defend the doctrine against these so-called new insights.

It is certainly not my purpose to enter this debate. I mention it because Christians should be aware that subtle modifications of this kind may, in due time, cause a significant shift in the church's teaching, such as it is, at the grass roots. The best defence against any perversion of the truth is to gain a thorough working knowledge of the Scriptures on the subject.

In his work on justification, John Owen, the Puritan divine who was often involved in controversy, said: 'I lay more weight on the steady direction of one soul in this inquiry, than on disappointing the objections of twenty wrangling or fiery disputers' (*The Works of John Owen*, The Banner of Truth Trust, 1976, vol. 5, p.3). These are my sentiments exactly. The purpose of my work is to help those who want to find peace with God, and to assist believers to improve their understanding of this glorious doctrine. By doing so they will strengthen their assurance of eternal life.

Thankfully, what the Bible teaches may be believed without any reference to the current disputes. 'This is what we speak,' says Paul, 'not in words taught us by human wisdom but in words taught by the Spirit, expressing spiritual truths in spiritual words' (1 Cor. 2:13). We believe Paul was speaking the truth under the guidance of the Spirit, whose expertise in conveying that same truth to the mind of the believer far exceeds that of the cleverest of men.

Indeed, if the Holy Spirit does not enlighten the mind, we shall make no progress. Prejudice against the truth naturally thrives in unbelieving minds, whatever their academic ability. But for those who know and love the truth, the doctrine of justification by faith can never be merely a matter of academic interest.

Of course, it is possible to have knowledge of the truth in the mind without knowing the power of it in our lives. We may be conversant with Paul's teaching without knowing peace with God. When the Scripture speaks about understanding the truth, it means much more than having data in the mind. For example, when Jesus opened the minds of the disciples so that they could understand the Scriptures (Luke 24:45), he did much more than free up their brains.

The word 'mind' in Scripture does not merely refer to the grey matter. It includes the heart as well.

We should never forget that our faith does not rest on man's wisdom, but on the power of God (1 Cor. 2:5). 'The man without the Spirit does not accept the things that come from the Spirit of God, for they are foolishness to him and he cannot understand them, because they are spiritually discerned' (1 Cor. 2:14).

It follows that those of us whose minds and hearts have been opened to the truth, have a duty to make the most of our privileges. The blessings springing from our increasing knowledge are innumerable. The standard of our Christian living, our inner peace, and our assurance of eternal life are all affected.

A book of this kind would not be complete without a warning about those who try to use the doctrine of justification as a warrant for antinomianism — the notion that, since all our sins are blotted out, we are free from any obligation to keep God's law. We can do whatever we like!

Paul is clear on the matter. Sanctification — the word used in Scripture to describe the believer's growth in holiness — follows justification just as surely as day follows night. The glory of the New Covenant is this: God writes his laws on our hearts and gives us a desire to obey them (Jer. 31:33-34). Therefore, all who are justified by faith will have a desire to be like Jesus, our perfect example. If that is not the case, any claim to be justified by faith is manifestly false.

Let us then, especially those of us who teach, be careful in our study of God's word. If any aspect of the doctrine of justification is not clear in our minds, the fog must be cleared before we open our mouths. We need to remember that we who teach will be judged more strictly (James 3:1).

Finally, I make a plea to those readers who reject the doctrine to think about their position. Please consider what will become of you on the Day of Judgement. If you are not trusting in Christ, how will you plead? For no-one living is righteous before God (Ps. 143:2), and he does not leave the guilty unpunished (Exod. 34:7).

To avoid awkward phrases, I address the reader as male, but no discrimination is intended.

My sincere thanks to Joanne Eaves for her constructive criticisms and meticulous checking of the manuscript.

1.

Facing the truth

But your iniquities have separated you from your God;
your sins have hidden his face from you... (Isa. 59:2)

Don't deceive yourself

I was rushed into hospital with a severe pain in my chest.
After a thorough examination, the consultant put me on the
waiting list for an angiogram. The man in the next bed was
much younger and clearly in a serious condition. He was
constantly gasping for breath and complaining about the
severity of the pain. After a couple of days, however, pre-
sumably in response to medication, he began to feel a little
better and told me that he intended to go back to work.

An hour or so after he made this comment a doctor arrived. I overheard her explaining to the patient that because
of his serious condition, an ambulance had been ordered to
take him to another hospital for an immediate angiogram. In
spite of his slight improvement, the hospital authorities were
obviously unhappy about the man's condition and were
determined to find the underlying cause of the problem.

To my astonishment, the man refused to go. 'I am grateful
for what you have done,' he said, 'but am feeling much better
and cannot see the need to stay in hospital any longer.' The

doctor was not pleased. 'You are being very foolish,' she said in a stern tone. 'You are very sick and we must find out what's wrong.' 'I am very grateful for what you have done,' the patient repeated, 'and there's no need to detain me any longer.' After about ten minutes, during which time neither party showed any signs of giving way, the interview ended abruptly. The doctor left the ward clearly showing her vexation, and the man discharged himself later the same day.

I am no physician, but one look at the man was enough to convince me that he was taking a huge risk. I shared the doctor's feeling of helplessness. Here was a patient, diagnosed as very sick and in the right place to receive the appropriate treatment, and yet he chose to reject the advice of those who knew better than he. He was unnecessarily and wilfully deceiving himself. It was tragic.

But how much more tragic when we adopt this attitude to our spiritual sickness! Millions do. Many do so even when they are fully aware of God's diagnosis of their spiritual condition and what needs to be done to cure it. They deliberately reject the salvation God offers and choose to trust in their own assessment of themselves. And since the death of the soul is far more serious than the death of the body, nothing could be more foolish.

The guilt of those who behave in this way is often aggravated by the fact that deep down, they know all is not well but they go on pretending it does not matter. Some are even privileged to see the change the gospel has made in the lives of others and still choose to ignore it. The stark reality that death may overtake them at any moment, when it will be too late to do anything about it, is pushed to the back of their minds.

If you are not in this category but have a sincere desire to find peace with God, you should know that you are already in a privileged position. Do everything you can to take advantage of it. If you know a church within reach where the Bible is taken seriously and the gospel faithfully proclaimed —

a rare thing in some places these days — make the most of it. Persist in your quest and take no notice of those who tell you not to take yourself too seriously, or who tell you not to worry because you are a Christian already. Do not believe those who insist that there are many ways to God and that one religion is as good as another. These are the devil's lies.

The words of Jesus put an end to all argument: 'I am the way and the truth, and the life. No-one comes to the Father except through me' (John 14:6). Millions have found the way, and more are doing so every day. Be assured then that those who truly seek the Lord will surely find him. The promise God made to his people Israel stands for all time: 'You will seek me and find me when you seek me with all your heart' (Jer. 29:13). Nothing less will do.

If, on the other hand, you have no sense of need whatever or have convinced yourself that you are good enough to stand before God in your own right, I have nothing further to say. You would probably not be reading this anyway. It is very interesting to notice how Jesus dealt with people like this. To the self-righteous Pharisees he quoted this proverb: 'It is not the healthy who need a doctor, but the sick' (Matt. 9:12).

What did he mean? Was he telling them that they were not sick? Not at all. Like millions in our world today, they were desperately sick spiritually, but they did not think so. Jesus was telling them that his primary concern was for those who know their plight and recognize their need of him. He came to satisfy those who 'hunger and thirst for righteousness' (Matt. 5:6). For those who were so conceited as to think they were righteous enough, he had only words of rebuke.

When the Pharisees saw that Jesus dined with tax-collectors and 'sinners', they were horrified. How dare he defile himself by eating with dishonest and immoral people? (The Pharisees regarded those who collected taxes for the Roman occupying power as traitors. The word 'sinners' was used to describe common and immoral people.) How little these religious men knew their *own* hearts. And how inconsistent they were — so careful about their rituals and yet so proud of themselves.

What has changed? Just as when Jesus was on earth, self-righteous church folk still think of themselves as good enough for God. They resent any suggestion that they are spiritually sick and, therefore, God's demand for repentance doesn't apply to them. In spite of the fact that the name of Jesus is often on their lips in church, they want nothing to do with him, except perhaps to despise those who truly love him.

I have known many people like this. They will agree with the necessity of conversion, but only for those 'bad' people outside the church — people who have had a poor upbring-ing or have kept bad company — adulterers, muggers and murderers. Like the man who discharged himself from the hospital, they are not prepared to face the truth about their own condition which is every bit as serious.

Both inside and outside the church, the notion is abroad that sin no longer matters. It is just a flaw in human behaviour that affects everyone. Better education, better conditions and a little self-control will put it right. There is nothing to worry about.

It is astonishing how many still believe this lie. In a world that is torn apart by human sin, a world in which millions suffer as the direct result of man's depravity, it beggars belief. As standards of education have gone up in our country, standards of morality have gone down. That better conditions cannot cure the basic flaws in human nature is simply a matter of observation. Man can make rockets that overcome the downward pull of gravity but he is powerless to overcome the downward drag of sin. Governments, too, are powerless to stop the rot. In their blindness, they often speed up the process.

For those who are more discerning, however, sin is seri-ous. It separates a man from his God and leads to eternal death. The verdict of Scripture is clear: 'all have sinned and fall short of the glory of God' (Rom. 3:23), and 'the wages of sin is death' (Rom. 6:23). This is the disturbing truth! But how much better to be uncomfortable with the truth than consoled by a lie.

But how do we get the message across? No amount of clever argument or persuasion is adequate. Only God the Holy Spirit can do it. When he opens a man's eyes to see the danger he is in, that man will abandon all trust in himself and will want to know how to be put right with God. Eternal condemnation will confront him like a yawning chasm and his yearning for deliverance will take precedence over everything else.

Don't be deceived

The doctor in the hospital was doing her best to persuade the sick man to face the truth about his condition. He would not listen. He was deceiving himself. There are many people, however, who allow themselves to be deceived by others. If what they are told meets a perceived need, they will accept it without asking any questions.

Even those who are sincerely searching for the truth are often perplexed by the lack of agreement in the church as to what the truth is. Ministers who tell their people what they want to hear heavily outnumber those who are determined to be faithful to the word of God. The Scriptures contain a solemn charge to preach the word of God but most ministers do not treat it seriously. Some do not even know what it means. Others go further and deny the gospel altogether. Indeed, I have known members of the clergy who are not even sure about the existence of a personal God!

When it comes to the serious matter of where a dying person will spend eternity, many ministers are prepared to lie through their teeth. They are supposed to be God's servants and ministers of the word, and yet they are willing to tell a godless person at the end of his life that all is well. Then, at the funeral, they will tell the equally godless relatives that their loved one has gone to heaven. How do these ministers sleep in their beds? They are blind leaders of the blind (Matt. 15:14).

In view of the apostle Paul's prediction, we should not be surprised at this. Writing to young Timothy, he says: 'I give you this charge: Preach the Word; be prepared in season and out of season; correct, rebuke and encourage — with great patience and careful instruction. For the time will come when men will not put up with sound doctrine. Instead, they will gather around them a great number of teachers to say what their itching ears want to hear' (2 Tim. 4:1-3).

Those who are wise, however, will search the Scriptures for themselves to make sure that what they are told is the truth. They will not take anything for granted. This is a good thing to do even if we are sure that the teacher is a man of the Bible. Jesus said: 'If you hold to my teaching, you are really my disciples. Then you will know the truth, and the truth will set you free' (John 8:31-32).

I was called to visit a middle-aged woman who was suffering from terminal cancer. Before I went into the bedroom where she was lying, I was told in no uncertain terms by her relatives not to say a word about her serious condition. But I soon discovered that the woman was not going to be so easily deceived. Before I had been in the room five minutes, she said: 'I am glad you have come because I know *you* will tell me the truth. Am I going to get better?' As requested, I did not say a word about her condition but the woman was wise enough to know from what I did *not* say that she was near the end. She probably knew anyway.

My hope and prayer for you, the reader, is that you will have the courage to face the truth. Leave no stone unturned in your quest. If you have a Bible, check everything ministers of the church say, including me. If you do not have one, buy one as soon as possible and read it. If you are prepared to accept God's guilty verdict on your life, you have already taken a significant first step.

'The LORD looks down from heaven on the sons of men to see if there are any who understand, any who seek God. All have turned aside, they have together become corrupt; there is no-one who does good, not even one' (Ps. 14:2-3). If these words trouble you, remember it is God's verdict. He does not see as man sees. In his eyes, nothing that we do is as good as it should be. If you are now ready to face the truth about yourself, then thank God for the progress you have made.

2.

The human problem

The heart is deceitful above all things and beyond cure.
(Jer. 17:9)

Natural hostility to God's law

Yes, if you are ready to face the truth, especially the truth about your guilty status before God, you have taken a huge step in the right direction. You are now in a position to understand the need for justification. If we can make a comparison between natural birth and spiritual rebirth (John 1:13), we could say that the head of the baby is already born and the rest of his body will quickly follow. The rest should not be so painful either.

The reason why so many baulk at this point is to be found in the human rebellion against God. Unless God's Spirit is at work, this hostility makes it impossible for us to accept his verdict. It is not just that some choose to resist him and some do not. We are all afflicted. Left to our own devices, we are beyond cure.

Paul's words are conclusive: 'The mind of sinful man is death, but the mind controlled by the Spirit is life and peace; the sinful mind is hostile to God. It does not submit to God's law, nor can it do so. Those controlled by the sinful nature cannot please God' (Rom. 8:6-8). There is no middle way. Either we have the Holy Spirit within us to show us where we stand, or we do not.

To preach this to the congregation in many churches today is likely to provoke a strong reaction. The gospel is not flattering to human nature generally, but to self-righteous church people it is particularly offensive. Reaction to it may take the form of outright but silent rejection, or open hostility against the preacher. No preacher enjoys this reaction, but it is his solemn duty to proclaim 'the whole will of God' (Acts 20:27). I remember at least three occasions when I was physically threatened after preaching along these lines. Of course, this proves what the apostle is saying. God's truth is distasteful to all in whom the Spirit of God is not at work. 'The man without the Spirit does not accept the things that come from the Spirit of God, for they are foolishness to him, and he cannot understand them...' (1 Cor. 2:14).

I was recently introduced to a Polish woman who did not speak English. I greeted her warmly and for some unknown reason she must have assumed I spoke fluent Polish. She smiled at me as if to say, 'At last I can talk to someone in my own language.' It must have been about a minute before I could stop her, and when she realized I had not understood a word of it she looked crestfallen.

So it is when the gospel is explained to someone, religious or otherwise, in whose heart the Spirit of God is not at work. He may hear the words but they do not mean anything to him. This is why I say to you, if you have come to the point where you freely acknowledge your guilt in the sight of God, you have clear evidence that the Spirit of God is at work in your life.

Your next step is to obey God's command to repent (Acts 17:30). Remember that all those who refuse to repent and believe the good news of the gospel are already under condemnation. Jesus said so in the clearest of terms: 'Who-ever believes in him is not condemned, but whoever does not believe stands condemned already because he has not believed in the name of God's one and only Son' (John 3:18). The unbeliever need not wait for a further 'guilty' verdict. It has already been passed and only true faith in Christ can reverse it.

The ability to repent is God's gift, but he never withholds it from those who long to know him. If, on the other hand, we are aware of the salvation God offers and still refuse to repent and believe, our punishment will be all the more severe. 'Anyone who rejected the law of Moses died without mercy on the testimony of two or three witnesses. How much more severely do you think a man deserves to be punished who has trampled the Son of God under foot, who has treated as an unholy thing the blood of the covenant that sanctified him, and who has insulted the Spirit of grace?' (Heb. 10:28-29).

These words need a little explaining. The 'covenant' is the new covenant, or as we call it, the New Testament. The 'blood of the covenant' is the blood of Christ who is the Mediator of the new covenant. The words mean that when those who have been 'sanctified' (set apart by having the privileges of Christian teaching and probably by making some form of commitment) reject the gospel, they are guilty of insulting God the Holy Spirit. There is no act of wickedness more serious than this. We shall come back to the covenant in chapter fourteen.

Guilt

I can imagine some reader saying: 'You have been going on about sin since the beginning of the book, and now you talk about guilt. Have we not had enough?' It is true that Bible-believing Christians are often criticized for harping on about sin and guilt. 'Why don't you talk about something a little more cheerful?' people ask. 'Do you not realize that feelings of guilt can cause depression or worse?'

Yes, of course we do. But we are not talking about feelings of guilt that are the result of a nervous disorder of some kind. In such cases, it is possible to feel guilty when there is nothing to feel guilty about. Guilt that comes through knowing we have not kept God's law is something entirely different.

Not one of the many people I have known who passed through the painful experience of feeling guilty before God went to see their doctor. Like the Prodigal Son (Luke 15:11-24), they knew very well what the problem was and who they were dealing with. The Prodigal's resolve to go back to his father and say: 'Father, I have sinned against heaven and against you' was a necessary lead up to the great rejoicing that followed.

In any case, it is not true to say that Christians are always talking about sin. We emphasize it because the Bible emphasizes it. The Christian life is one of triumphant joy and we talk about this much more. We speak about sin and guilt for the same reason that the doctor tells his patient what is wrong with him. For if the patient does not know, he is not likely to take the pills.

In the same way, true joy will never be ours until we acknowledge our guilt and turn to Christ in repentance and faith. Many centuries before Christ was born, Isaiah said: 'He was pierced for our transgressions, he was crushed for our iniquities; the punishment that brought us peace was upon him, and by his wounds we are healed. We all like sheep, have gone astray, each of us has turned to his own way; and the LORD has laid on him the iniquity of us all' (Isa. 53:5-6). Not only does this predict the sufferings of Christ, but it explains their purpose as well.

The same prophet tells us about the universal proclamation of the gospel and the invitation to all who are thirsty, to come and drink freely of the satisfying waters: 'Come, all you who are thirsty, come to the waters; and you who have no money, come buy and eat! Come, buy wine and milk without money and without cost' (Isa. 55:1). The glorious salvation God offers is free.

To understand the doctrine of justification by faith we should be aware that the Bible has two main parts, the Old Testament and the New Testament. Many people mistakenly think that the Old Testament is all about God's law and the New Testament all about the gospel. Some even go further and think in terms of the cruel God of the Old Testament and the loving Jesus of the New. This is a false impression. Rather, anything in Scripture that is in the form of a moral command from God is his moral law, whether in the Old or the New Testament, whilst anything that relates to subjects like God's forgiveness, justification by faith, reconciliation and so forth, is gospel.

The above quotations from the Prophecy of Isaiah are an excellent example of the gospel in the Old Testament. The words of Jesus recorded in Matthew 5:17-18 give clear evidence of the law in the New: 'Do not think that I have come to abolish the Law or the Prophets; I have not come to abolish them but to fulfil them. I tell you the truth, until heaven and earth disappear, not the smallest letter, not the least stroke of a pen, will by any means disappear from the Law until everything is accomplished.'

Since the Reformation in the fifteenth and sixteenth centuries, it has been customary to regard the law and the gospel as two distinct parts of Scripture — the whole of Scripture. God's law tells us what standard God requires in our thoughts, words and deeds. It also tells us that we cannot reach the standard it lays down and, therefore, the law condemns us. God's gospel tells us how we may be delivered from the condemnation of the law and reconciled to him.

Is it not obvious, then, that in order to know our need of Christ we must first understand the nature and purpose of God's law? For where there is no knowledge of God's commandments, there can be no awareness of transgression. And where there is no awareness of transgression, there can be no sense of guilt, no repentance and no appreciation of divine forgiveness.

The curse of the law

Curses are usually associated with witchcraft, voodooism and false religions. Their authenticity cannot be proved because the evidence is always circumstantial. Yet, in spite of this, many people are more than willing to believe that they are under a curse of some kind. If this were not the case, clairvoyants would soon go out of business. Advertisements, like the following by a certain Alinda Bartlett, would be pointless: 'Do you ever feel that things around you are not going quite right no matter what you do or do you think someone has cast a Jinx spell or wished harm on you? ... Alinda will personally make up your chosen spell individually just for you. This requires a great deal of work, love, care and time. Please don't be fooled by cheap and poor quality imitations. Alinda's spells are of the highest quality. She has many clients coming back from all over the world for repeat spells. Many have commented on the positive results they have had & the beauty and quality of her spells.'

The idea of God cursing anyone, however, is shocking. Yet this is exactly what he has done. In the Israel of the Old Testament, God required the priests to recite to all the people in a loud voice a long list of curses. They all begin with the words 'Cursed is the man who...' They fall on those who carve images, dishonour their parents, move their neighbour's boundary, lead the blind astray, have illicit sexual relations, commit murder and accept bribes. They are summed up in these words: 'Cursed is the man who does not uphold the words of this law by carrying them out' (Deut. 27:14-26).

'Ah but,' some will say, 'these were tribal laws for an ancient people.' Certainly not. The curse is renewed in the New Testament where the apostle Paul says: 'All who rely on observing the law are under a curse, for it is written: "Cursed is everyone who does not continue to do everything written in the Book of the Law"' (Gal. 3:10). But there is a subtle difference here. The curse now rests on those who *rely* on their observance of the law.

How unkind and unloving, we say. How can a God of love curse anyone? But this is precisely our problem. The evil tendency within us inclines us to reject God's verdict. God does not say very nice things about sinners like us and we don't like it. Creating a god who is more to our liking is an efficient way of easing the conscience. It is also a sure way to eternal destruction.

In any case, as we shall see in a moment, in his great love for us God has made provision in Christ for the curse to be removed. If, however, we spurn his offer of mercy and forgiveness, the curse remains. Those who think they can get to heaven by keeping God's law will be bitterly disappointed.

So two alternatives are now plainly set before us. We may try to gain God's favour by what we do, or we may acknowledge our transgressions and trust wholeheartedly in what Christ has done for us. If we take the first road, the curse remains. If we take the second road, the curse will be lifted.

This is the Good News of the gospel: Christ has done what we could not do. He 'redeemed us from the curse of the law by becoming a curse for us, for it is written: "Cursed is everyone who is hanged on a tree"' (Gal. 3:13; Deut. 21:23). Under the Law of Moses, criminals were put to death by stoning and their bodies hanged on a tree. This was a sign of divine rejection. The fact that Jesus was 'hanged on a tree' meant that he died under the curse — the curse of my sin — and was, therefore, rejected by his Father. Hence his bitter cry from the cross: 'My God, my

God, why have you forsaken me?' (Mark 15:34). Who can plumb the depths of his agony?

The shocking nature of these Scriptures has driven some to try to water them down. But this is like trying to take the heart out of the gospel. It serves no purpose. The teaching of Jesus and Paul on this subject is indeed offensive. But what greater folly can there be than to allow our loathsome pride to cloud our judgement in this way?

The future for those who are under the curse is grim indeed. To those who showed their opposition to his mission by refusing to help his disciples, Jesus said: 'Depart from me, you who are cursed, into the eternal fire prepared for the devil and his angels' (Matt. 25:41). What can be more shocking than this? Yet it would be better if we had never been born than to ignore it.

As we have seen, if we try to secure forgiveness from God through our own efforts, by attempting to keep his law, we are doomed to failure. The only 'righteousness' that is acceptable to God is his own. This is the righteousness that he credits to us through faith, 'for all have sinned and fall short of the glory of God, and are justified freely by his grace through the redemption that came by Christ Jesus' (Rom. 3:23-24).

There was no other good enough to pay the price of sin;
He only could unlock the gate of heaven, and let us in.

(Cecil Frances Alexander, 1818-1895)

3.

God's unwritten law

Indeed, when Gentiles, who do not have the law, do by nature the things required by the law, they are a law for themselves, even though they do not have the law, since they show that the requirements of the law are written on their hearts... (Rom. 2:14-15)

God's unwritten law

Near the village of Tebay in Cumbria, several men were working on the main line railway track. A low bogey wagon loaded with short lengths of steel railway lines was hurtling towards them at forty miles an hour. It was out of control. Since the men were using machinery and it was dark, they neither saw nor heard the truck coming. About two miles up the track, other workers had loaded the wagon, and because its brakes had been tampered with, it began to roll slowly and silently. Due to the steep gradient, it picked up speed and struck the men. Four were killed.

What caused the accident? The failure of the brakes on the bogey is the immediate answer. To be more precise, was it not neglect on the part of the man whose job was to maintain the brakes? Of course, it could also be said to be the law of gravity, one of the forces that make brakes necessary.

A less serious incident had beneficial results. Isaac Newton was sitting under an apple tree when an apple fell on his head. The bump apparently triggered something in his brain because he suddenly came up with the Universal Law of Gravitation! At least that is how the story goes. If there is any truth in it, it is probably more likely that the falling apple confirmed the conclusion he had already reached.

The great thinker realized that if the force of gravity reached to the top of the highest tree, might it not reach as far as the moon. Putting it in simple terms, Newton concluded that if a missile could be fired into space at the right velocity it would circle the earth. Earth's gravity would pull it downwards but it would never hit the ground because the earth would be moving at the same time. If the moon behaved in the same way, it would explain why it orbited the earth.

One does not have to be a physicist to understand that God's creation is governed by laws such as these. We may not understand the science behind them but the way many of them work — gravity, magnetism, motion, for example — is simply a matter of observation.

Those who are determined not to see God's hand in creation, invent many theories to explain how these laws came into existence. Those who are wiser see them as reflecting 'God's invisible qualities — his eternal power and divine nature' (Rom. 1:20). For those who believe in creation — as all who rely on the Scriptures do — natural laws are God's laws.

Strictly speaking, they are not laws at all, but principles of operation built into creation. They do not change and cannot be ignored without suffering the immediate consequences. The law of gravity, for example, makes no allowances for human stupidity. Even so, such stupidity cannot be called sin because there is no suggestion of personal accountability to another person. If I put my finger in the fire, it would be a stupid rather than an immoral act.

God's Moral Law, which we shall consider in the next chapter, is of a very different order. It is not something we have discovered by observation but is revealed to us in Scripture. As we shall see, ignoring God's law is not merely disregarding a principle of operation. In this case, it is a sin against a Person, and that Person is God himself. The penalty is certain but not necessarily immediate.

Not far from my home are some of the highest cliffs in England. They rise to a height of a hundred and twenty five metres. In several places, there is a sheer drop into the sea. Those who climb the fence and go too near the edge run the risk of falling. Not too long ago two teenagers did just that and lost their lives. Obviously there are no signs warning people about the law of gravity — what we call 'descriptive law' — but because some people are foolhardy there are several signs to remind sightseers that climbing the fence is prohibited. This is what we call 'prescriptive law'.

Without prescriptive law, it would be impossible for us to live together in a community. If, for example, I choose to ignore the law that says I must drive on the left side of the road, chaos would result. If a builder chooses to ignore the building regulations, trouble will ensue. Some years ago, a builder decided to use empty petrol cans instead of bricks to save money. They could not be seen under the plaster. The block of flats he erected collapsed, killing many people.

In spite of the voices that ask why, we are all under obligation to obey laws prescribed by the state. The apostle Paul makes it very clear: 'Everyone must submit himself to the governing authorities, for there is no authority except that which God has established ... he who rebels against the authority is rebelling against what God has instituted, and those who do so will bring judgement on themselves' (Rom. 13:1-2).

This too may be regarded as God's law because it is no exaggeration to say that Scripture regards civil government as God's institution (Rom. 13:1). If we do not obey the law of

the land, we disobey God. Paul goes so far as to say that our
duty in this matter is both moral and civil. In other words, if
we fiddle the tax return or break the speed limit, we are guilty
of sin because indirectly we are breaking God's law.

There are big differences, however, between civil and divine law. Civil law is constantly changing to meet changing
circumstances, but God's Moral Law never changes. Civil law
can be brought into disrepute. In some cases, it has to be
abandoned because it cannot be enforced. God's Law,
however, can never be brought into disrepute and is never
abandoned. Millions escape conviction where breaches of the
law of the state are concerned and miscarriages of justice are
common. No one escapes divine justice and miscarriages are
impossible.

Sometimes, governments pass laws that contravene God's
law. Many Christians face this problem in various parts of the
world. We read in the Acts of the Apostles that the Sanhed-
rin — the highest tribunal of the Jews — issued an order to
Peter and John not to speak any longer in the name of Jesus.
Without hesitation they replied: 'Judge for yourselves whether
it is right in God's sight to obey you rather than God. For we
cannot help speaking about what we have seen and heard'
(Acts 4:19-20).

Quite right too! No government has the authority to inter-
fere with the law of God. If it does, then believers have a
solemn duty to disobey. Jesus himself laid down the principle:
'Give to Caesar what is Caesar's, and to God what is God's'
(Matt. 22:21). In this land of ours, state law was once based
on God's law, but this is no longer the case. And the more we
move away from the authority of God's Moral Law and allow
immoral pressure groups to influence legislation, the more
likely it becomes that Christians will be under obligation to
break the law. And the more the state authorities will be
exposed to the judgement of God.

There is no shortage of people who want to base civil law
on what they call 'natural law'. When used in this sense, the

term refers to theories that exclude God altogether. Members of the Natural Law Party in the United States, for example, claim to be able to use the 'intelligence' in evolution for the benefit of the human race. By this means, they claim, perfection similar to that observed in the working of the universe may be achieved in our social life. Conversely, all the evils that plague our society are caused by our failure to use this method!

As far back as Thomas Aquinas, a philosopher and theologian who lived in the thirteenth century, the notion of natural law was being considered. For an argument to be valid, he argued, it must start from facts observed in the natural world. Since human reason is both the measure and rule of human actions, we should all know how to behave in a reasonable manner! (I wonder what went wrong.) Indeed, according to natural law theories, every law about morality can be demonstrated to be either right or wrong. Therefore, we can build a system of moral laws just by observing nature!

With all the different godless theories we have today, it would be impossible to agree on what morality really is. The joke about optimistic people having misty optics certainly applies to all who accept these theories. They all fail to take into account the Biblical doctrine of Original Sin — man's natural tendency to rebellion against the law of God. This inherited tendency makes the attainment of perfection in this life impossible. Thankfully, we are not at the mercy of the philosophers but have been provided with clear moral guidelines in the word of God.

The law of conscience

I remember my father paying £24 to the taxman — a large sum in those days — because he had a conscience about it. The Inland Revenue said he did not owe the money but he was so sure they were wrong, he paid up! The term 'conscience money' is usually reserved for those who, unlike my father, have an uneasy conscience about fiddling their tax returns. In order not to be discovered, they pay what they think they owe anonymously.

In the Old Testament, we read that David, the future King of Israel, 'was conscience-stricken' (1 Sam. 24:5). King Saul with three thousand chosen men went out to find David, his sworn enemy. The king went into a cave to relieve himself, not knowing that further in the cave David and his men were hiding. When they saw that Saul was at David's mercy, they urged him to kill the king but David could not do it. Instead, he crept forward and cut off a corner of Saul's robe. Even then, David's conscience did not approve.

In the New Testament, Paul argues that 'it is necessary to submit to the authorities, not only because of possible punishment but also because of conscience' (Rom. 13:5). Here, a conscientious submission to the law of the land is seen as our duty to God.

The word 'conscience' comes from Latin and is made up of two words meaning 'knowledge alongside' or 'co-knowledge'. It is that part of our make-up that passes judgement on our words and actions. The Scriptures teach us several important truths about the conscience.

The most important thing we learn is that the conscience passes judgement on our actions according to God's moral law. For, says Paul, when Gentiles 'do by nature the things required by the law, they are a law for themselves, even though they do not have the law, since they show that the requirements of the law are written on their hearts, their consciences also bearing witness, and their thoughts now accusing, now even defending them' (Rom. 2:14-15).

Since we are all made in God's image, it is only to be expected that we have a good idea what God requires even if we have never heard of the Ten Commandments (Rom. 2:14-15). For example, the man who honours his parents is being obedient to the fifth commandment even though he may not know it. His conscience approves. By the same token, the man who is ignorant of the seventh and tenth commandments, forbidding adultery and covetousness, but runs off with his neighbour's wife knows he is doing wrong. His conscience disapproves.

None of this means that the conscience is completely reliable as a judge of our actions. Even so, it should not be ignored. Apart from the written law of God, men have no other means to determine what his demands are. We shall see in a moment that the Scriptures are the only entirely reliable judge of our behaviour. They are also our best teacher. When God's word is written on the heart (Rom. 2:14-15), the conscience is far better informed and much more efficient.

On the other hand, the consciences of those who 'reject the truth and follow evil' (Rom. 2:8), become less efficient. They may even become cauterized, 'seared as with a hot iron' as Paul puts it (1 Tim. 4:2). Such consciences become callous and insensitive to the point where they are virtually ineffective.

We may be tempted to think that those who are ignorant of God's written law have an advantage because the standard set by the conscience may not be as high as that set by the Ten Commandments. This is not so. The fact is that everyone is inexcusable. Those who do not have God's law fail to keep their own standards just as badly as those who do have it, fail to keep God's. In any case, ignorance of God's law is never an advantage to anyone. We shall come back to this important point in Chapter Five.

4.

God's written law

All who sin under the law will be judged by the law.
(Rom. 2:12)

Uses of the word 'law' in Scripture

Parkinson's Law is well known. C. Northcote Parkinson wrote
a satirical book in which he maintained that the sum total of
work done is always in inverse proportion to the number of
workers. In a business enterprise the point is reached where
more workers may mean less work. Again, the word 'law'
here means a principle of operation.

I too have a 'principle of operation'. I call it 'Frank's Law'
because I imposed it on myself: 'You shall rest after a meal'.
Let me explain. If I do anything strenuous after a meal these
days, I get a pain in my chest. Because this has gone on for a
long time, it has become an established principle. My wife will
tell you that I am not strict enough in observing the 'law'. She
is quick to remind me when she senses that I am about to
infringe it.

The word 'law' is sometimes used in Scripture in a similar
way. In Romans 7:21, for example, Paul says: 'So I find this
law at work: When I want to do good, evil is right there with
me.' Like every true believer, Paul's best intentions were

always thwarted by the presence of evil in him, so he saw it as a law. We find a similar use of the word in Romans 8:2, where the apostle refers to the gospel as 'the law of the Spirit of life'. The gospel gives life because the Holy Spirit is the author of it. This is an unalterable principle of operation and, therefore, a law.

The word 'law' may also be used in a general sense to include everything that reveals God's will. When David prayed, 'Open my eyes that I may see wonderful things in your law' (Ps. 119:18), he was not thinking only of God's commandments. The whole of Scripture as he knew it was in his view.

In other places, however, the word is more confined. It sometimes refers to the Old Testament but excluding the writing of the prophets, as in the expression 'the Law and the Prophets' (Rom. 3:21). In some places, particularly in the passages where Paul is explaining the doctrine of justification by faith, the word is mainly restricted to the Ten Commandments (Gal. 3:17).

Broadly speaking, where the word 'law' has its more usual meaning — commands that must be obeyed — there are three categories. This threefold division is helpful because it separates out those aspects of divine law that are relevant to our study of justification by faith. These categories are known as Moral, Civil and Ceremonial. The Moral Law refers principally to the Ten Commandments. The Civil Law relates to the application of laws in specific circumstances. The Ceremonial Law governed the ritual of the sacrificial system of the Old Testament when the church was in its infancy.

The Ceremonial Law is to be found mainly in the Book of Leviticus. Primarily, it was for the guidance of the priests when performing their rituals in the tabernacle and later, the temple. Since the Ceremonial Law was temporary, it has no further application to the church, except that we do learn a lot about the way in which it is fulfilled in the Person and the sacrifice of Christ.

The writer to the Hebrews makes this clear. Referring to the Ceremonial Law he says: 'The law is only a shadow of the good things that are coming — not the realities themselves. For this reason it can never, by the same sacrifices repeated endlessly year after year, make perfect those who draw near to worship' (Heb. 10:1). He also explains that when Christ, our High Priest, had offered for all time one sacrifice for sins, he sat down at the right hand of God. His one sacrifice has made perfect forever those who are being made holy (Heb. 10:12,14).

Even in the Old Testament, before the coming of Christ, evidence for the precedence of God's moral commands over ceremonial observances is easy to find. Samuel the prophet said to King Saul: 'This is what the LORD Almighty says: "I will punish the Amalekites for what they did to Israel when they waylaid them as they came up from Egypt. Now go, attack the Amalekites and totally destroy everything that belongs to them"' (1 Sam. 15:2-3). But King Saul spared King Agag and the best of the sheep and cattle. When Samuel accused Saul of failing to obey, he made the excuse that the sheep had been kept alive so that they could be used as sacrificial offerings to God. Samuel replied: 'Does the LORD delight in burnt offerings and sacrifices as much as in obedience to the voice of the LORD? To obey is better than to sacrifice...' (1 Sam. 15:22; see also Hosea 6:6 and Prov. 21:3).

The same point is made by Jeremiah: 'Hear, O earth: I am bringing disaster on this people, the fruit of their schemes, because they have not listened to my words and have re-jected my law ... Your burnt offerings are not acceptable; your sacrifices do not please me' (Jer. 6:19-20). The failure of the people to obey the Moral Law made their ceremonial rituals offensive to God. Matthew Henry observes: 'a careful conformity to moral precepts recommends us to God more than all ceremonial observances' (*Exposition of the Old and New Testament*, J. Nisbet & Co.).

The division is even sharper in the New Testament. Paul insists, for example, that the ritual of circumcision counts for nothing apart from obedience to the Moral Law. To the Jews he says: 'Circumcision has value if you observe the law, but if you break the law, you have become as though you had not been circumcised' (Rom. 2:25). Therefore, if Jews break the Moral Law, circumcision will be of no advantage to them. (We could say the same about those who are outwardly members of the Christian church but who have no regard for God's law.)

Some laws were enacted in ancient Israel that are no longer applicable; laws relating to the inheritance of land in Canaan, for example, or the law about raising up children for one's deceased brother. Indeed, there were many laws given to the Jews that did express the will of God for them, but only in the particular circumstances in which they found them-selves. When the circumstances changed, the laws no longer applied. Since it is not too difficult to see the difference between the temporary laws and the permanent ones, this should not present a problem.

Enough has been said to show that the concept of 'Law' in Scripture is complex. Therefore, it will come as a relief to the reader to know that our main concern in this book is with the purpose and function of God's Moral Law, and that neither is difficult to understand.

The authority of God's moral law

As part of my training, I had to attend a series of lectures on 'moral theology' in Manchester Cathedral. The lecturer, a Cathedral Canon (a title given in the Church of England to one of the officiating ministers in the Cathedral), told the assembled company that the Ten Commandments no longer applied in today's world. There is now no such thing as an inflexible and unchanging law, he insisted. Right and wrong must be determined by the circumstances prevailing at the time.

Before this lecture, the Canon had led the service of Morning Prayer in the Cathedral. Using the 1662 Book of Common Prayer, he said to God on behalf of everyone present: 'Almighty and most merciful Father, we have erred and strayed from thy ways like lost sheep, we have followed too much the devices and desires of our own heart, we have offended against thy holy laws...' To say that this was a classic case of hypocrisy would be putting it mildly. He confessed before God that we had all violated his commandments, which are, of course, inflexible and unchanging, and half an hour later, he was telling his pupils that they do not exist.

The next training day, the absurdity of the Canon's views was exposed in a dramatic fashion. I was late for Morning Prayer. Arriving at the Cathedral with about half-an-hour to spare, I could not find a parking space. The Cathedral car park was reserved for Cathedral staff and was already full, as were all the streets in the vicinity. I drove round and round in ever-increasing circles before I found a place, but it was then about a twenty-minute walk back to the Cathedral.

After the service, we assembled in the ante-room for the lecture in the usual way, but we were first given a lecture of a different kind, and it was obviously directed at me. 'It seems to me,' said the Canon, 'that some of you are averse to worship. Please be sure you arrive on time in future.' I was not pleased. Why, I wondered, did the man assume that my lateness proved my aversion to worship? And why did he not have the decency to ask why I was late before launching into this public rebuke?

Still hurting during the lecture, I lost concentration. I began to think that if there is no such thing as a moral absolute, why did I bother to find a legal parking place? If God's command to Christians to obey the government (Rom. 13:1) no longer applies, why did I not ignore the law and park on double yellow lines? Mind you, the police would probably have had a different opinion. So if, as the Canon had insisted, moral actions must be determined by the circumstances, who had the authority to determine where I should park my car — the Canon, the Police, or me?

Thankfully, I did not have the problem. Since God's Law says that we should obey the authorities, then my first duty was to obey the traffic laws. As we saw in Chapter Three, obeying the law of the land is not a matter of private opinion, but a moral duty we owe to God. It is one of God's inflexible and unchanging laws.

Let it be admitted that determining the right course of action in complex circumstances is not always easy. But this does not mean that when we are faced with two evils, the lesser evil becomes good, even when circumstances force us to choose it. Since God is perfect, it follows that his laws are perfect. Therefore, what is right and what is wrong does not vary. Imagine the problems that would arise if we had the responsibility of deciding in what circumstances we were free to break God's commandments!

The well-known story about the young Jew who lied to protect his mother is sometimes used to support the Canon's position. The Gestapo knocked on the door and demanded to know if she was at home. She was hiding in the attic, but her son, knowing she would almost certainly end up in a concentration camp, lied to protect her. I think we would all agree that lying was better than betrayal in such a case, but that does not make lying right. Circumstances may make wrong necessary, but they never make it right. 'Woe to those who call evil good and good evil, who put darkness for light and light for darkness' (Isa. 5:20).

The fact that these situations do occur does not, therefore, mean that there are no moral absolutes or that what is right is determined by the circumstances. A white lie is still a lie and a breach of the ninth commandment. In any case, far too much is made of these extreme cases. Those who know God and are familiar with his commands have little difficulty in knowing what their daily duty is.

The Lord Jesus was explicit in his view of the authority of God's Moral Law: 'Do not think I have come to abolish the Law or the Prophets; I have not come to abolish them but to fulfil them. I tell you the truth, until heaven and earth disappear, not the smallest letter, not the least stroke of a pen, will by any means disappear from the Law until everything is accomplished' (Matt. 5:17-18).

Indeed, Jesus teaches us that the law has a deeper application than we may have thought, reaching down to the evil desires of the heart. The sixth commandment forbidding murder also applies to unjustified anger: 'You have heard that it was said to the people long ago, "Do not murder, and anyone who murders will be subject to judgement." But I tell you that anyone who is angry with his brother will be subject to judgement' (Matt. 5:21-22). He does the same with the seventh commandment that forbids adultery: 'Anyone who looks at a woman lustfully has already committed adultery with her in his heart' (Matt. 5:28).

The attitude of Jesus to the Scriptures is summed up in these few words: 'The Scripture cannot be broken' (John 10:35). Jesus did not mean that the Law of God cannot be disobeyed. On the contrary, we all disobey it. He meant that the Scriptures could not be annulled. The arguments and philosophies of men may be made null and void but not the word of God.

The purpose of God's moral law

The Moral Law was intended to impress upon the Children of Israel the holiness and righteousness of their God. It still serves the same purpose for us, but we have the advantage of having the highest possible revelation of God's holiness in the Person of Jesus Christ. His life was a demonstration of the Moral Law in action, for he was the holy and righteous one (Acts 3:14). If we want to know what God is like in all his perfection, we must look to Jesus.

Nevertheless, God's Moral Law is permanent and changeless. Since God's nature does not change, and his Law is rooted in his nature, it follows that our duty to him does not change either. Therefore, unlike the law of the state, our duty is to a Person rather than a law. The law of the land is not the Queen's Law or the Prime Minister's Law because both are subject to it. Our duty to obey state law cannot directly take the form of accountability to a person. God's Moral Law always does.

This duty embraces love to both God and neighbour. The Ten Commandments are divided into two parts — the first four setting out our duty to God and the last six, our duty to others. The two parts are closely connected, however. If we do not put God first for example, as the first commandment requires, we shall find it much more difficult to refrain from covetousness, as the tenth commandment requires. The opposite is also true because if we do not love our brother, how can we possibly love God? (1 John 4:20).

In particular, we should understand that God's commandments are not written to spoil our pleasure. He did not say to himself: 'I have decided to put restrictions on human beings so that they will not enjoy themselves too much'. Indeed, it is the transgression of his law that brings unhappiness. Actually, God did not decide anything. As we have already seen, the command to his creatures to love him and worship him and not to commit murder, adultery and theft is not the result of a resolution on his part. It is the natural expression of his nature. His perfect character is the absolute standard of righteousness and this is revealed in his commandments.

The universal application of the Moral Law is set out at the beginning of the Bible in the Genesis narrative. Adam was created a moral human being under divine law. He was the head of all people and under the terms of the agreement God made with him, perfect obedience was required. Adam was on probation (Gen. 2:17). As a reward for perfect obedience to God's law as it was revealed to him, Adam and his descendents were promised everlasting happiness. Should he fail, however, God's wrath would come upon them and they would be placed under the curse (Rom. 5:12). This arrangement with Adam, sometimes called the Covenant of Works, is really a forerunner of the Ten Commandments.

Three principal uses of the Moral Law have been clearly identified. These too are helpful. The first and most obvious is that it tells us what God requires. It deters sin and promotes righteousness. If this were its only purpose, the outlook would be grim because we all fall short of the standard God has set (Rom. 3:23).

Secondly, it makes us conscious of our sins and of our inability to comply with its demands. This consciousness is a necessary preparation for the gospel: '...through the law,' says Paul, 'we become conscious of sin' (Rom. 3:20). 'I would not have known what sin was except through the law. For I would not have known what coveting really was if the law had not said, "Do not covet"' (Rom. 7:7).

Thirdly, the Moral Law remains a rule of life for all believers. When Paul claims that believers are free from the law, he means that we are free from the condemnation of the law. He does not mean that we are free from the obligation to obey it. We now look briefly at the three uses.

1. The law restrains wrong and promotes right

Whether under a dictatorship or an elected government, no society can survive without law. It serves an essential purpose in promoting peace and restraining evil and changes to meet changing circumstances. God's Moral Law is also essential for the same reason, but it never changes because it deals with the responsibilities of human beings to God, and these are always the same.

The Moral Law prescribes rules for morality in a way that state law can never do. Its principles go deeper because it lays down rules for behaviour in areas of our lives that are beyond the reach of state law. For example, it would be impossible for any government to introduce legislation to prevent a breach of the tenth commandment — you shall not covet — because offences could not be proved. Again, if a person is guilty of failing to love his neighbour as himself, as God's Law prescribes, it is outside the jurisdiction of any human judge. The state may prescribe laws that prevent a person from harming his neighbour, but that is as far as it can go.

Just as traffic laws are necessary to restrain dangerous behaviour and promote safe travelling on the nation's roads, so God's Moral Law is necessary to restrain sinful behaviour and promote righteousness and justice. The other day I read about a woman who drove her BMW at a hundred miles an hour down the fast lane of a motorway on the wrong side of the road. Imagine what chaos that could have caused! We do not need great powers of imagination, however, to realize the moral morass that disregard for God's Moral Law produces. We see it on every hand. The suffering that sin causes is limitless.

Therefore, if we are to be a civilized society, the restraining influence of the Moral Law of God is necessary. Indeed, it comes under the heading of what theologians call 'Common Grace', a label that is used to refer to God's goodness in preventing evil from running rampant in the world. The authority of governments to promote peace and prosperity is a good example. Although there may be corruption and serious errors in their policy-making, the general intention of their actions is for the peace and security of society. There are exceptions of course, but they do not annul the general principle.

The title 'Common Grace' arises from the fact that it applies to every living person. It also distinguishes common grace from 'Special Grace', the grace that applies only to those whom God has chosen. Obviously, due to the widespread ignorance of God's Commandments in our nation today, their restraining influence is weaker than it used to be. Nevertheless, we should be thankful for God's grace in this area, although in a book about justification by faith we need not consider it further.

None of this means that God's Law is bad. Because the Law defines what sin is, it is so easy to think of it as creating sin. It can certainly provoke sin, because perverse human beings are often tempted to do what they are told not to do. When I was a child, the first thing I wanted to do when I saw a 'No Trespassing' notice, was to climb the fence. It is well known that many children enjoy the excitement of stealing — until they are caught. And judging by the young men who drive their cars past my door, the speed restriction sign provokes them to put their foot down.

Paul himself talks about sinful passions being 'aroused by the law' (Rom. 7:5). But he is careful to explain that it is not the fault of God's Law but of our sinful nature. After telling us, in the verse quoted earlier, that he would not have known what sin was except through the law, he now explains that the same law intensified his sinful desire: 'For I would not have known what coveting really was if the law had not said, "Do not covet". But sin, seizing the opportunity afforded by the commandment, produced in me every kind of covetous desire' (Rom. 7:7-8.). The good law produced evil, but only because it aggravated man's rebellion against it.

2. God's moral law makes us conscious of sin

I am a diabetes sufferer. At my last six-monthly check-up, the nurse who carried out the test told me about one of her patients who refuses to accept that his condition is serious. Consequently, he is careless about taking his medication and he does not stick to his diet. Since this attitude is common, the local health authority has been making a special effort to convince diabetic patients of the seriousness of the disease.

It is clear from the first three chapters of Paul's letter to the Romans that he understood the reluctance of human nature to accept God's diagnosis of our spiritual disease. For this reason, he too makes a special effort to make his readers understand the desperate nature of their condition. Otherwise, they will not be particularly interested in the remedy.

The question is: have we understood it? Are we willing to face up to the fact that God's law condemns us, or are we still comparing ourselves with other human beings and feeling good about ourselves — like the Pharisee who looked down on the tax-collector and gave thanks that he was not like him? (Luke 18:11). I have met many people who comforted themselves by doing this — and a few others who, like the ostrich, put their heads in the sand in the hope that God could not see them.

The stark truth is this — we shall never have a desire to know God unless and until we accept the fact that we are hell-deserving sinners in his sight. We shall never know what it means to be justified by faith unless and until we accept God's verdict that we are guilty.

A very simple way of realising this is to think seriously about Christ's summary of the law. It is contained in the answer Jesus gave to a Pharisee, 'an expert in the law,' who 'tested him with this question: "Teacher, which is the greatest commandment in the Law?" Jesus replied: "'Love the Lord your God with all your heart and with all your soul and with all your mind.' This is the first and greatest commandment. And the second is like it: 'Love your neighbour as yourself.' All the Law and the Prophets hang on these two command-ments'" (Matt. 22:35-40).

These words should silence for ever the claims of those who think of themselves as righteous in God's sight. Jesus is telling us that if we keep these two commandments, the rest will follow. If we love God with all our being, we shall never take his name in vain. If we love our neighbour as much as we love ourselves, we shall never steal from him or covet his wife. But who in his right mind would claim to have main-tained this standard?

It follows then, that in spite of the fact that God's Law is good, all it can do is condemn us. 'Now we know,' says Paul, 'that whatever the law says, it says to those who are under the law, so that every mouth may be silenced and the whole world held accountable to God' (Rom. 3:19).

'Moses describes in this way the righteousness that is by the law: "The man who does these things will live by them"' (Rom. 10:5). That is to say, if we were able to keep the law 'twenty four seven' as we now say — every moment from the cradle to the grave — we would indeed be justified by our own deeds. Apart from Jesus Christ, however, 'the man who does these things' does not exist. No wonder Paul calls it 'the law of sin and death' (Rom. 8:2).

When the Spirit of God applies the Moral Law to us in our natural and unbelieving state, the experience is both gruelling and glorious. It is gruelling because deep conviction of sin shatters our false hopes and opens to our gaze the appalling destiny of the wicked. I have known people weep for weeks under the rod of God's Law. God had revealed to them the true state of their hearts and they did not like what they saw. Yet, such conviction is the first step on the road to glory. This is what Paul means when he says, 'The law was put in charge to lead us to Christ that we might be justified by faith' (Gal. 3:24). The law is in charge in the sense that it shows us where we have gone wrong and what the penalties are.

It is glorious because when God brings us 'out of darkness into his wonderful light' (1 Peter 2:9), it is like coming out of a long dark tunnel and seeing the glory of God's creation bathed in sunlight. Our eyes are opened to see the beauty of Jesus and, through him, we are able to look with our new eye of faith to the glory to come. As the apostle Peter puts it, it is 'an inexpressible and glorious joy' (1 Peter 1:8).

The joy of seeing the beauty of Jesus and of anticipating the glory to come, coincides with our justification. Paul puts it like this: 'Therefore, since we have been justified through faith, we have peace with God through our Lord Jesus Christ, through whom we have gained access by faith into this grace in which we now stand. And we rejoice in the hope of the glory of God' (Rom. 5:1-2).

3. God's moral law remains a rule of life for all believers

The people whom God has justified by faith through the death of Christ are under a particular obligation to obey God's law. I stress this because the pernicious idea is abroad that once justified, Christians have no such obligation. The people who believe this fatal notion are known as Antinomians. The word is a combination of two words: 'anti' meaning 'against' and 'nomos' meaning 'law'.

Since this evil is never far away, true believers should be constantly aware that justification offers no escape from the duty to keep God's commandments. Of course, we shall not be able to achieve perfect obedience and our shortcomings will be covered by the death of Christ. Nevertheless, God's law remains the standard to which we must aspire.

Some critics insist that free justification weakens one's resolve to keep God's law. But this is the judgement of those who have no practical experience of these things. In fact, it does precisely the opposite. The antinomianism of people who claim they are Christians may be seen by the critics as evidence to support their view. The only thing it proves, however, is the bogus nature of the antinomians' claim. The person who knows he is justified will quickly discover that knowing God is always accompanied by a strong desire to glorify him. The only way to do this is to live a holy life. In Bible terms, sanctification must follow justification.

The word 'sanctification' has a double meaning. It describes the believer's status in that he is now set apart for God. In my home, we have a jar that is labelled 'Salt'. It is set apart from other jars for the exclusive purpose of storing salt. In a similar way, believers are set apart from the rest of humanity for God's exclusive use. In Jeremiah 1:5 we read these remarkable words: 'Before I formed you in the womb I knew you, before you were born I set you apart; I appointed you a prophet to the nations'. The older Authorized Version reads: 'I sanctified thee, and I ordained thee...' This setting apart certainly takes place in God's mind before we are born. The knowledge of it comes as soon as we are justified.

More importantly for our present purpose, the word refers to the believer's moral improvement — his growth in holiness and righteousness. This is the work of the Holy Spirit in the believer's life. It is the gradual demolition of the old way of life, and the building up of the new. The demolition and the building take place together. Sanctification, therefore, is both a fact and a process and both follow justification as surely as day follows night.

Our growth in holy living depends a lot on the regular use of Holy Scripture. The reason why Christians grow at different speeds is not hard to find. Those who rarely read the Bible are slow developers, tossed to and fro by doubts. Those who feed regularly on it grow quickly and have a strong assurance. 'Like newborn babes, crave pure spiritual milk, so that by it you may grow up in your salvation, now that you have tasted that the Lord is good' (1 Peter 2:2-3).

5.

God's universal justice

Will not the Judge of all the earth do right? (Gen. 18:25)

His unchanging justice

During the time of the English Commonwealth, moss-troopers roamed around the Scottish border looking for what they could steal. Many of them were deserters from the army who kept their weapons and became bandits. They were called moss-troopers because they used the mossy growth along the border to hide. In those days, certain privileged individuals inherited local jurisdiction and interpreted justice as they saw fit. When the bandits were caught, they were executed in the border town of Jedburgh and tried later. This procedure became known as 'Jeddart Justice'.

The English counterpart of this barbaric practice is known as 'Abingdon Law'. It is said that in 1644-45, Major-General Browne of Abingdon hanged his prisoners and tried them in court afterwards.

These are by no means isolated incidents. In the Second World War and other conflicts since, perpetrators of mass murder have escaped justice. Even in peace time, the administration of justice is constantly under threat. Some depraved individuals will stop at nothing in their attempt to pervert the

course of justice. They hire false witnesses and bribe juries.
Even the police are sometimes found to be corrupt. One
wonders just how many innocent people are languishing in
jail and how many unconvicted murderers are walking the
streets.

Thankfully, efforts are ongoing to keep ahead of the anarchists. Changing circumstances, too, make it necessary to
update the law and plug loopholes. The Civil Justice Council,
an advisory body for England and Wales, has the task of
monitoring the civil justice system, and promoting its modernization. The need for such a body is obvious. Yet in spite
of these checks, there is constant need for vigilance to try and
ensure that new laws are fair to all parties.

In sharp contrast, God's universal justice remains unchanged and unchangeable. He does not need anyone to
monitor his justice system or to promote its modernization.
The 'Judge of all the earth' (Gen. 18:25) does not shift his
position on the punishment of sin. Why? Because he does not
change and human nature does not change.

God's universal justice, like his righteousness, is natural to
him. Indeed the only difference between the two is that the
former is the application of the latter. To put it another way,
his justice is the natural response of his righteousness to evil in
all its forms. The prophet Habakkuk puts it like this: 'Your
eyes are too pure to look on evil; you cannot tolerate wrong'
(Hab. 1:13). God will not clear the guilty (Exod. 34:5-7)
because he cannot.

The perfection of God's nature guarantees that on the Day
of Judgement there will be no miscarriages of justice and
nothing will be overlooked. 'But I tell you', Jesus said, 'that
men will have to give account on the day of judgement for
every careless word they have spoken' (Matt. 12:36). Those
who uttered the careless words may have long since forgotten
them, but they are all recorded in the mind of God. Unlike
human judges, God is all-knowing and, therefore, is always in
possession of all the facts. The writer to the Hebrews is

emphatic: 'Nothing in all creation is hidden from God's sight. Everything is uncovered and laid bare before the eyes of him to whom we must give account' (Heb. 4:13). 'It is unthinkable that God would do wrong, that the Almighty would pervert justice' (Job 34:12). The millions of past injustices that no one can do anything about have not escaped his searching eye.

His justice may be long delayed but it is never set aside permanently. The rich may prosper and the poor get poorer. Suicide bombers may continue to put themselves out of reach of human justice, and the guilty may still be set free while innocent people languish in prison. The sceptics' cry may still be heard, 'if there is a God out there, why does he allow these injustices to continue?'

This complaint has been made ever since the fall of Adam. Even God's servants are perplexed by the injustices in the world. The Scriptures provide us with many examples. The prophet Jeremiah was a faithful servant of the Lord and convinced of his righteous judgment. Yet, he felt the injustices of his day deeply. 'You are always righteous, O LORD, when I bring a case before you. Yet I would speak with you about your justice: Why does the way of the wicked prosper? Why do all the faithless live at ease?' (Jer. 12:1).

The prophet was treated so badly by his own people just for telling them the truth that he began to wish he did not exist: 'Cursed be the day I was born! May the day my mother bore me not be blessed ... why did I ever come out of the womb to see trouble and sorrow and to end my days in shame? (Jer. 20:14,18).

Godly Asaph, too, complained to his God about the wicked being carefree and wealthy. He even began to wonder whether living a holy life was worth it: 'Surely in vain have I kept my heart pure; in vain have I washed my hands in innocence' (Ps. 73:13). But the despair did not last. 'When I tried to understand all this,' he said, 'it was oppressive to me till I entered the sanctuary of God; then I understood their final destiny' (Ps. 73:16-17).

Injustice is not easy to live with. The person who is not troubled by it is totally lacking in compassion. But although we are not able to solve all the problems, we rest in the sure knowledge that justice will certainly be done. For God '...has set a day when he will judge the world with justice by the man he has appointed. He has given proof of this to all men by raising him from the dead' (Acts 17:31). God has not told us when that day will dawn, but he has made it very clear that his Son will be the Judge and not a single sin will be over-looked.

The conscience as arbiter of justice

In Chapter Three we considered the law of conscience, that innate sense of right and wrong that is part of our make-up because we are made in the image of God. Although the image has been marred by sin so that our natural sense of justice is flawed, we still have a good idea of what is right and wrong. For those who do not know the Ten Commandments, the conscience becomes the only arbiter of justice. Yet, on this basis alone, the vast majority of people have a sense of fair play. The people who would approve of Jeddart Justice, for example, are still few and far between.

An interesting question arises here. Why, do you think, the majority would condemn practices like Jeddart Justice and Abingdon Law? If we were to describe them as examples of the murky depths to which 'justice' can sink, few would disagree. But why do we see them as essentially wrong? Is it not because there is in our make-up that reflection of God's character we talked about earlier? In most of us there is still an awareness of our accountability to God.

There is no cause for complacency, however. The number of those who see morality as a matter of opinion is increasing fast. At the same time, protests against miscarriages of justices and light sentences for serious crimes seem to get louder. Inconsistencies like this are inevitable when we move away from God's law. The public conscience becomes less efficient as a result.

The recent findings of those who claim to specialize in the origins of criminal behaviour provide us with another example. Atmospheric pollution and poor nutrition, they say, is partially to blame for bad behaviour! Now of all the theories about the causes of crime this must surely take the prize for triviality. Where is the evidence that those who live in pure air and eat well are less likely to break the law? Whatever link there may be between crisps and crime, the principal cause is being ignored. A corrupt and deceitful heart is not cured by fresh air or by a better diet (Jer. 17:9). Eating more vegetables is not a crime buster. 'This is what the LORD Almighty says ... They dress the wound of my people as though it were not serious' (Jer. 6:9,14).

The only way, therefore, to change bad behaviour is to change the heart and only God can do this. 'I will give them an undivided heart and put a new spirit in them; I will remove from them their heart of stone and give them a heart of flesh. Then they will follow my decrees and be careful to keep my laws. They will be my people, and I will be their God' (Ezek. 11:19-20).

Going back to Frank's Law for a moment — digging the garden after a big meal irritates an already existing condition and causes me pain, but it does not cause the condition. If I stop digging, it will not repair my damaged heart. In the same way, if we put all the crooks in the world on a healthy diet and send them on a cruise, it will not turn them into saints. Sin is a heart disease, not a diet problem.

His justice demonstrated in the death of Christ

This world has never seen, nor will it ever see, a more appalling act of injustice than the sentence of death passed on the
pure and sinless Son of God. He 'committed no sin, and no
deceit was found in his mouth. When they hurled insults at
him, he did not retaliate; when he suffered, he made no
threats. Instead, he entrusted himself to him who judges
justly' (1 Peter 2:22-23). The facts speak for themselves. The
Lord Jesus was not guilty of anything and yet, after a mock-
ery of a trial, he was condemned to death on a Roman cross.

Strange as it may seem, nor will this world ever see a more
perfect demonstration of justice. Paul tells us that God presented his Son as the one who would turn aside his wrath 'to
demonstrate his justice at the present time, so as to be just
and the one who justifies those who have faith in Jesus'
(Rom. 3:26). It is important to understand what Paul is saying
here. Through the death of Christ, God demonstrates that he
is righteous in forgiving guilty sinners. Justice and mercy
embrace each other and God is vindicated. The Judge of all
the earth cannot be just in justifying guilty sinners unless the
penalty is paid. He cannot justify those who do not have faith
in Jesus. It would be a gross injustice to do so.

It is not enough to believe that Christ died for the sins of
the world. It must become personal. We must be able to say
with the apostle that the Son of God 'loved me and gave
himself for me' (Gal. 2:20). From early childhood I believed
that Jesus died for the sins of the world, but it made no
difference. Peace with God came only when I realized that it
was for *my* sins that he died. He is *my* Saviour.

What amazing love! What richness of mercy! The one who
is deeply offended because of my sins has reconciled me to
himself. What an absurdity it would be, what an affront to the
mercy of God if, in the light of this astonishing privilege, I
were to protest my innocence! What a fool I would be to

claim that my own miserable self-righteousness is acceptable to God! Such ridiculous claims are made only by those who are ignorant of God's free and undeserved grace.

In some circles, the fact that God gave up his sinless Son to death to satisfy his righteous demands is seen as immoral. 'Where is the justice in the innocent dying for the guilty?' they cry. The teaching that Christ was our Substitute is rejected out of hand. They do not have a leg to stand on, however. In many places, the Scriptures speak of God's wrath against sinners as necessary and inevitable. Take Ezekiel 7:8, for example: 'I am about to pour out my wrath on you and spend my anger against you; I will judge you according to your conduct and repay you for all your detestable practices'.

No doubt, the long-standing objection to the idea of substitution arises from the fact that there is nothing in our experience of life to compare it with. Where human justice is concerned, I am not permitted to give my life in place of someone on death row. To get someone released from prison by paying his debts is the nearest we can come to it. With God, however, we are in a different situation altogether. No sinful human being could take the punishment for my sin because he too is guilty. Only someone from heaven, perfect in every way, could do it.

On the question of substitution, the Scriptures could not be clearer. The Old Testament sacrifices that pre-figured Christ's 'once for all' sacrifice were a substitute for the life of the person making the sacrifice. For example, God told Moses that the offerer 'is to lay his hand on the head of the burnt offering, and it will be accepted on his behalf as an atonement for him' (Lev. 1:4). Of the sacrifice of Christ, the apostle Peter says: 'For Christ died for sins once for all, the righteous for the unrighteous, to bring you to God' (1 Peter 3:18).

What these objectors seem not to understand is that the three Persons of the Trinity — Father, Son, and Holy Spirit — are all involved in the plan of redemption. The Father gave his Son in accordance with his eternal purpose; the Son was willing to execute his Father's plan, and the Holy Spirit applies the benefits of the Son's death to those whom he chooses. The Father delights in the Son. God has 'exalted him to the highest place and gave him a name that is above every name' (Phil. 2:9). The Son delights in the Father whom he loves. 'The world must learn', Jesus said, 'that I love the Father and that I do exactly what my Father has commanded me' (John 14:31). In view of this, in what way could the Father be unjust to his beloved Son?

To come back to the point, God's demands being fully satisfied on our behalf, the apostle John is able to say that God is both 'faithful and just' to forgive our sins (1 John 1:9). He could not be faithful to his promise to have mercy on us if his Son had not died. The debt would have remained outstanding. But now he is both true to his promise and true to his justice.

The outcome for the believer is glorious. Paul puts it concisely: 'Therefore, there is now no condemnation for those who are in Christ Jesus' (Rom. 8:1). We need to see what Paul is *not* saying in this breathtaking statement. He is most certainly not saying that those who belong to Christ do not deserve condemnation. Nor is he saying that everyone in the world is now free from condemnation. The two words 'no condemnation' describe the believer's permanent position and no one else's. He is now in a right relationship with God and no power in the universe can change it. Christ has paid the penalty for the sins of his people once and for ever. No further sacrifice is necessary. God cannot be guilty of the injustice of demanding punishment twice over — once from his beloved Son and again from the believing sinner.

It is important to stress that by his death, the Lord Jesus Christ has procured everything we need for our complete deliverance from the penalty and power of sin. Nothing, absolutely nothing, remains to be done. Christ has fulfilled all the conditions of our salvation. As the 1662 Prayer Book of the Church of England puts it, Christ made 'a full, perfect, and sufficient sacrifice, oblation and satisfaction, for the sins of the whole world...' (Communion Prayer of Consecration).

The standard of justice

We come now to the question as to what God's standard of justice is, and whether there will be different standards for different kinds of people. The Scriptures recognize two standards. One for those who know God's law and another for those who do not. 'All who sin apart from the law,' says Paul, 'will also perish apart from the law, and all who sin under the law will be judged by the law' (Rom. 2:12). Obviously, since the knowledge of God's commandments varies from person to person, there will be many people who fall somewhere between the two standards.

Different standards, however, do not hold out the hope that some may be justified by their deeds. Whether we are judged by divine law or the human conscience, God's guilty verdict remains and it is perfectly just: 'All have sinned, and fall short of the glory of God' (Rom. 3:23). 'There is no-one righteous, not even one' (Rom. 3:10). 'If you, O LORD, kept a record of sins, O Lord, who could stand?' (Ps. 130:3). For the unbeliever, the punishment of sin is inevitable.

As we saw earlier, under the law of the state, ignorance is no excuse. Indeed it cannot be. The offender would only have to say 'Sorry, I didn't know' and he would be excused. Several times in my life, when in a town I was not familiar with, I have driven the wrong way down a one-way street without knowing. In almost every case, the locals were quick to shout and wave their arms frantically to save me from falling into the hands of the police.

Where God is concerned, however, if we do not know we are doing wrong, he does not hold it against us. Jesus laid down the principle: 'That servant who knows his master's will and does not get ready or does not do what his master wants will be beaten with many blows. But the one who does not know and does things deserving punishment will be beaten with few blows. From everyone who has been given much, much will be demanded' (Luke 12:47-48).

'Good!' someone may exclaim, 'I will remain ignorant! It will be easier for me on the Day of Judgement.' Alas, it is a forlorn hope. Like everyone else in this world, those who do not know God's word still have a clear revelation of God's character in nature and they choose to ignore it. For 'what may be known about God is plain to them, because God has made it plain to them. For since the creation of the world God's invisible qualities — his eternal power and divine nature — have been clearly seen, being understood from what has been made, so that men are without excuse' (Rom. 1:19-20). In any case, wilful ignorance is a serious offence in itself.

It comes as a surprise to many believers, that we are not to be judged by what we know or what we believe, but by our deeds alone. What we have said and done will be the only criteria. The same standard will apply to kings and queens as well as to their lowest subjects. It will apply to the rich and famous, as well as to the poor and unknown. Paul is clear: 'God "will give to each person according to what he has done"' (Rom. 2:6). 'For we must all appear before the judgment seat of Christ, that each one may receive what is due to him for the things done while in the body, whether good or bad' (2 Cor. 5:10).

How can this be? If we are justified by faith and not by deeds, how can we be judged according to our deeds and not our faith? Let me explain. After the premature death of Martha's brother, Lazarus, Jesus said to her: 'I am the resurrection and the life. He who believes in me will live, even though he dies; and whoever lives and believes in me will never die' (John 11:25-26). This clearly teaches that a person is saved by faith alone apart from works (Rom. 4:6). Indeed, no greater promise has ever rejoiced the hearts of men.

It may seem strange, then, that Jesus also teaches that the servant who behaves badly will be severely dealt with when his master returns, and will be assigned a place with the unbelievers (Luke 12:45-46). Paul, too, tells us that God will give eternal life to 'those who by persistence in doing good seek glory, honour and immortality' (Rom. 2:7). It would appear that we have an irreconcilable contradiction.

Let us think of a person whose knowledge of the Bible is comprehensive, and whose faith in its truthfulness and reliability is unshakeable. If that person does not show any of the marks of the new birth (John 3:3) — love for God and neighbour, love for God's word, love for God's people and a willingness to spend one's life in the service of Christ — what sort of faith does he have? It is all in his head, leaving his heart unchanged.

By contrast, let us think of a person who embraces the gospel with enthusiasm and whose lifestyle is changed for the good to some extent. But like the seed that was choked by the thorns, 'the worries of this life and the deceitfulness of wealth choke it, making it unfruitful' (Matt. 13:7,22). This is not genuine faith either. The change is not permanent.

Who, then, are the people with genuine saving faith? In other words, who are the people who seek glory, honour and immortality by persisting in doing good? Is it not the people whose faith is demonstrated by a life of devotion to God to the end of their days? Whoever heard of an unbeliever seeking glory, honour and immortality? As John Stott says 'perseverance is the hallmark of genuine believers' (*The Message of Romans*, Inter Varsity Press, p.84). Those who do not persist in doing good, in spite of their claim to have faith, are not true believers.

We need to be careful because what is genuine always has its counterfeit. According to Jesus, some people *think* they are serving the Lord but they will find themselves excluded from the kingdom: 'Not everyone who says to me, "Lord, Lord," will enter the kingdom of heaven, but only he who does the will of my Father who is in heaven. Many will say to me on that day, "Lord, Lord, did we not prophesy in your name, and in your name drive out demons and perform many miracles?" Then I will tell them plainly, "I never knew you. Away from me, you evildoers!"' (Matt. 7:21-23). For all their gifts, they are not doing the will of the Father.

When Jesus comes in his glory to judge the world, he will separate the righteous from the unrighteous just as 'a shepherd separates the sheep from the goats ... Then the King will say to those on his right, "Come, you who are blessed by my Father; take your inheritance, the kingdom prepared for you since the creation of the world..."' (Matt. 25:32,34). There can be no doubt whatever that these are the people whom Christ has saved by grace, who were known by him before the world began. What separates them from the rest? They serve the Lord and his people faithfully as long as they have breath (verse 40).

There is no comfort here for those who hope to be justified by their deeds. We are saved by faith alone, but faith that does not lead to godly living never saved anyone. It is dead. The only qualification God will accept from those who do not trust in Jesus, is a perfect life from beginning to end — perfect in thought, word and deed, every moment of every day. As long as we are in this body, perfection will remain unattainable.

But perfection will not be required of God's children on the Day of Judgement. The imperfections in their service for the Master are all graciously covered by the righteousness of Christ. For this reason, God sees them as perfect.

Take the example of the dying thief. He was obviously saved by faith alone because when he trusted in Christ he was breathing his last. It was the kind of faith that would have transformed his character if he had been given the opportunity. How do we know this? Because Jesus said to him, 'Today you will be with me in paradise' (Luke 23:43).

The dying thief is proof that even the good deeds that are the evidence of faith do not contribute to our justification. Our 'good' deeds, whether before or after justification, are simply not good enough. If God were to consider them when assessing our worthiness to enter his kingdom, we would not be allowed over the threshold.

God is no one's debtor. Even the faith by which we are justified is his gift (Eph. 2:8). Believers ought never to say (as many do) 'I am a Christian because I trusted in Jesus'. It is a half-truth, and half-truths are easily construed as untruths. Salvation is never a reward, not even for our trust. Faith is God's gift to all whom he chooses (Eph. 2:8). To the subject of faith we now turn.

6.

Saving faith is trust

*Now faith is being sure of what we hope for and certain of
what we do not see. (Heb. 11:1)*

In 1859, Jean Francois Gravelet (1824-1897), otherwise
known as Blondin, walked over the Niagara Falls on a tight
rope. The rope was 1,100 feet (335 metres) long and 160 feet
(49 metres) above the water and Blondin was pushing a
wheelbarrow. On one occasion, he even cooked and ate an
omelette half way across! On another occasion, so it is said,
he asked the people watching if they believed he could take a
man across in the wheelbarrow. Enthusiastically, they an-
swered 'Yes!' in chorus but, when he asked for volunteers, no
one came forward.

The story may have been added to over the years, but it
still serves to illustrate the difference between intellectual faith
and absolute trust. Everybody believed Blondin could do it,
but no one was prepared to climb into the wheelbarrow and
put his life on the line. They believed in their minds but the
element of trust was missing.

Trust is the essence of genuine faith — trust in God and in
the word of God. God's gift of saving faith not only gives birth
to a deep-seated conviction that both God and his word are
trustworthy, but also to a willingness to 'get into the wheelbarrow'. It is on the basis of this act of absolute trust in Christ that

God justifies the sinner. It follows, therefore, that all who have saving faith are saved. Merely knowing the truth of the gospel in the mind never saved anyone.

The person who is blessed with saving faith will quickly realize the gravity of his sins. He will stop making excuses for himself and he will know that, apart from Christ, there is no hope for him. Although he may not understand why, he will have the assurance that Christ died for him. He will also discover a willingness in his heart to do God's will, whatever that entails, and that implicit trust in God is the secret of a purposeful and consistent life.

To digress for a moment — the question as to whether assurance is of the essence of faith has long been a matter of controversy. That is to say, if we have saving faith, does it follow that we also have immediate assurance that we are saved, or is that inner certainty something faith acquires gradually as it develops? To put the question another way, are all believers confident of their heavenly inheritance, or just those whose faith increases by making the most of their opportunities?

The difficulty arises because of the uncertainty of the Greek word that is translated 'being sure' in Hebrews 11:1. In the Authorized Version, the word is translated 'substance'. Here are the two texts side by side: 'Now faith is the *substance* of things hoped for...'; 'Now faith is *being sure* of what we hope for...' Obviously 'substance' refers to something objective and real, something outside the believer's mind. In this case, the writer is saying something like this: 'Now faith makes real the things we hope for...' Our future inheritance becomes so real to us that we know we are already in possession of it. 'Being sure', however, describes a subjective conviction, something in the believer's experience.

It may be true to say that both amount to the same thing in the end because, if something I cannot see becomes real to me, then I am sure of it. Perhaps the word 'substance' is better because in these days many people claim to feel sure about all sorts of things that have no substance whatever.

Certainly, the Scriptures seem to teach that assurance *is* an essential part of faith, but is it true that every believer is immediately sure of what he believes? If his faith is weak, will his assurance not also be weak? Obviously, if his faith were free of doubt, he would be fully assured, but this is seldom the case. On the other hand, he may have a vague sense of security as soon as he trusts in Christ, but it may take time to understand and appreciate it. Every believer's experience is different.

The important thing for the reader to understand is that being certain of what we do not see is not a pipedream. It is the birthright of every Christian. Trust in the Christ of the Bible carries with it a conviction that salvation is all of God from beginning to end. Therefore, the believing sinner should be persuaded that God is not only the author of his faith, but also the one who sustains it and perfects it (Heb. 12:2).

The believer who knows what it means for the Spirit of God to testify with his human spirit that he is a child of God (Rom. 8:16) will readily concur. As I say in my book *How Can I Be Sure?* (Grace Publications), 'When the Spirit confirms our sonship in this way we are not left in any doubt about who is speaking and why. Those who have this inner assurance cannot question it. It takes them out of the realm of uncertainty and enables them to rejoice in their adoption as God's children. Those who do not have it cannot possibly know what we are talking about.'

To come back to the point, we need to be clear that when a man puts his trust in Jesus Christ, it is not blind trust. He does not say to himself, 'I will put my trust in this unknown Person and see if it works.' To trust someone we know nothing about is a risky business. Indeed, if it were not for the gracious work of the Spirit in our hearts and minds we would remain ignorant of Christ. We would never know enough about him to put our trust in him.

How then can we know? If we are privileged to hear preachers who are true to the Bible, we may learn from them. We may also know someone who has known the Saviour for many years and who will testify to his faithfulness. We may also learn from books, but as there is a lot of printed rubbish out there that claims to be Christian, we may need guidance. Our main source of knowledge is, of course, the Bible. If we are new in the faith and have no one to advise us, it is probably best to start reading John's Gospel carefully.

The object of justifying faith is Christ, and he is revealed to the teachable mind through the Holy Scriptures. We are not putting our trust in a book but in a Person. It is, of course, legitimate to think of the promises of God as the object of our trust, but this is because they are fulfilled in Christ. His substitutionary death guarantees their reliability. As Paul says: 'For no matter how many promises God has made, they are "Yes" in Christ' (2 Cor. 1:20).

When I was sixteen or seventeen I was introduced to that old song 'Standing on the promises of Christ my King'. The chorus repeats the word 'standing' several times. It helped me to understand the meaning of trust in God's word because we put our trust entirely in whatever we stand on. Recently a friend of mine stood on a stepladder to reach for something. The ladder proved to be untrustworthy and he ended up on the floor with broken bones.

The importance of trusting the word of Christ recorded in the Scriptures is stressed by John the Baptist. Speaking of Christ, John says: 'The one who comes from heaven is above all. He testifies to what he has seen and heard, but no-one accepts his testimony. The man who has accepted it has certified that God is truthful. For the one whom God has sent speaks the words of God, for God gives the Spirit without limit' (John 3:31-34).

This needs a little unpacking. John is saying that Christ is superior to every other human being because he is God. He is the one who tells the truth because he is the truth

(John 14:6) and has come from his Father in heaven. Very few people believe what he teaches, but the person who publicly declares his trust in the testimony of Jesus Christ has endorsed the fact that God is truthful. The Authorized Version is helpful here. It says: 'He that hath received his testimony has set his seal that God is true'. We are not talking about a literal seal, of course, but just as a man puts his seal on a document to indicate his acceptance of its contents, so the believer 'puts his seal' on the testimony of Christ recorded in Scripture. To the man who is unwilling to do this, justification by faith — if he knows anything at all about it — will be nothing more than a religious idea.

Ironically, many people find simple trust difficult. Usually it is because they entertain so many intellectual difficulties and want answers before they will believe. With God, such difficulties are inevitable because God is infinite and we are finite. Everything about him is beyond our ability to understand. '"For my thoughts are not your thoughts, neither are your ways my ways," declares the LORD. "As the heavens are higher than the earth, so are my ways higher than your ways and my thoughts than your thoughts"' (Isa. 55:8-9).

In very old buildings, the doorways are low. From time to time one sees a sign on the lintel that reads: 'Bend or Bump'. It is impossible to pass through the door without bending down. To move forward in faith, humility is essential. If we refuse to bend we shall get hurt. The reason for this is not hard to find. By trusting in Christ alone for my salvation, I am freely admitting that God is right and I am wrong. To submit to the righteousness of Christ (Rom. 10:3) means abandoning my own, of which I may have been so proud. The words of James are to the point: 'God opposes the proud but gives grace to the humble' (James 4:6).

I am reminded of doubting Thomas who was absent when the risen Christ appeared to the other disciples. When they told him that they had seen the risen Lord, he declared, 'Unless I see the nail marks in his hands and put my finger where the nails were, and put my hand into his side, I will not believe it'. A week later, Jesus appeared again but this time Thomas was present. Jesus said to him: 'Put your finger here; see my hands. Reach out your hand and put it into my side. Stop doubting and believe'. Jesus then said to him: 'Because you have seen me, you have believed; blessed are those who have not seen and yet have believed' (John 20:24-29).

These words are a warning to all who refuse to believe anything beyond their powers of reasoning. Oddly enough, they trust their doctor when he prescribes medicine for their ailments. They trust their teachers in order to progress in their particular field of learning. If they are businessmen, they trust the word of their colleagues, and so on. But when it comes to trusting Christ, they start demanding proofs for his teaching, proofs that they would never understand even if they were given. What folly! Jesus said: 'I tell you the truth, anyone who will not receive the kingdom of God like a little child will never enter it' (Mark 10:15).

Trust in Christ elevates a person to a position where he finds an inner strength beyond what is natural. As Isaiah puts it, 'those who hope in the LORD will renew their strength. They will soar on wings like eagles; they will run and not grow weary, they will walk and not be faint' (Isa. 40:31). The prophet is not saying that those who trust in the Lord are never tired. Rather, that we have resources available to us that enable us to triumph in everything this life may throw at us. Our confidence grows in strength and brings us through to the place where we can 'draw near to God with a sincere heart in full assurance of faith…' (Heb. 10:22).

7.

Saving faith is reasonable

Do not conform any longer to the pattern of this world, but be transformed by the renewing of your mind. (Rom. 12:2)

Faith is not fantasy

I am reliably informed that a group of clergy in the Isle of Man, whenever they travelled to Douglas for a meeting of the synod, were in the habit of stopping the car at the Fairy Glen. They wanted to pay their respects to the fairies! Over the years, I have been surprised — not to say shocked — by some of the antics of clergymen. So much so that I had reached the stage where I thought nothing would shock me. The story about the fairies, however, was so fantastic, I assumed it was a joke. Alas, it was all very serious.

To say that this kind of behaviour is a departure from common sense would be putting it mildly. The word 'stupid' would describe it more appropriately. Yet, the astonishing reality is that many people today, including some of the clergy, would not see anything amiss in believing in fairies. The 'reason' for this bizarre attitude is that anything to do with faith is now considered to be outside the scope of reason altogether. To subject anyone's faith to reasonable scrutiny is seen as an infringement of his rights. 'Believe what you like' is the order of the day, so that faith in fairies, gnomes or lepre-chauns or whatever else is legitimate if that is what we want.

So if Tom chooses to believe in 'God' as he likes to think of him, then that god is true for Tom. But what is true for Tom may not be true for me, and what is true for me may not be true for you. Indeed, if another ninety-seven people join us, each one believing in his own idea of what God should be like, we would have a hundred people with a god each. Ninety nine of these gods would not be true for Tom and the same number for you and for me. But if I think my God is the true God, it would be considered offensive to say so. I would be encroaching on your freedom to believe that your god is the true God.

I doubt if society has ever sunk to such a level of madness. No one in his right mind would apply this ridiculous notion to any other science. The mind boggles at the mere suggestion. Why then to theology, the queen of sciences? Yet, millions are content with it, not because it makes sense to them but because it cancels their accountability to the one true God. Those who take refuge in such crazy ideas should realize that there is only one God and it is to him that we shall all have to give account. When we die, our private gods will die with us.

To suggest, as some do, that we all believe in the same God but have different ways of thinking about him is absurd. In Old Testament times, the Ammonite people worshipped a god called Molech to whom they sacrificed their children. In modern times we have terrorists who believe in a god who, in their minds, calls them to murder people in their thousands. There is only one God (Deut. 6:4) and he condemns outright such violations of his holy law.

The notion that faith and reason are opposites has received a huge boost by this trend. It is assumed that we have no way of testing the genuineness or otherwise of a person's beliefs. Therefore, it would wrong for me to tell my neighbour that his faith is false. I might be wrong. But this is to commit intellectual suicide. What an insult to the human intelligence to suggest that it is not competent to make judgments where there is no proof. If our common sense tells us that what we believe is fantasy, we would be idiots to ignore it.

Thankfully, we have not all gone crazy. There are still people around who use their God-given brains to distinguish between truth and make-believe. True, as we have said before, the human intellect is not sufficient on its own to search God out, but this is not a reason to stop thinking.

Saving faith frees the mind

The bishop who presided at my ordination appeared to be a little irritated by my confidence in the Scriptures. He evidently thought that to take the Bible as my final authority in matters of faith was old-fashioned and narrow-minded. Several times he approached me and asked, rather rudely, 'Have you broadened your mind yet, Allred?' We have heard of people whose minds are so open that their brains are in danger of falling out. Judging by the bishop's performance whenever he opened his mouth in public, he was in danger of becoming one of them.

To reject the revelation of Holy Scripture in favour of the latest 'theological' fashion is not freedom as is supposed. It is a form of bondage that robs a man of his freedom, causing him to drift here and there wherever the prevailing current takes him. It also robs him of his security because the alternative to divine revelation is human speculation. What can be more perilous than to be blown about by every wind of teaching (Eph. 4:14)? By contrast, mental stability and the freedom to think as God intended us to do, is the consequence of submission to the truth.

Indeed, to submit the intellect to the word of God or, as Paul puts it, to 'take captive every thought to make it obedient to Christ' (2 Cor. 10:5), is necessary for salvation. To talk

about being justified by faith without accepting God's word as
trustworthy is nonsense. I am reminded of the story of the
man who stood on the street corner offering ten-pound notes
to passers-by. Most people walked past because they did not
believe him. They received nothing. Just a few believed the
man's word and were better off as a result. Unbelief is a sure
way to hell.

We have been suffering for years in the church at the
hands of scholars who seem to regard faith in God's word as
it stands as unreasonable. They presume to tell us which parts
of the Bible are true and which are not, and which parts
mean something different from what they say. Miracles in
particular are not allowed. Now what is this but a faithless use
of our reasoning powers? Those who use their brains in this
negative manner forfeit the aid of the Holy Spirit, and there is
no better reason for rejecting what they say. No matter how
clever we are, without the enlightenment of the Spirit we
cannot derive any spiritual benefit from the Scriptures
(1 Cor. 2:14).

Those who are blessed with saving faith are different. They
set their minds on what the Spirit desires (Rom. 8:5). They
submit to the word of God. And as they meditate on it, their
minds are fully and fruitfully engaged. Even if the Bible has
long been merely a matter of academic interest for them, it
can be so no longer. As the word comes alive, they realize
that the Spirit of God never gives power to the mind to
change the word, but he does give power to the word to
change the mind.

When the Spirit enlightens the mind, serious thinking always follows. This process begins as soon as the believer turns
to Christ and it sharpens his intellect to the point where its use
becomes an essential part of his service to God. Just as faith
develops by the use of the mind, so the mind is stimulated by
the exercise of faith. As we submit our intellect to the truth of
God's word, our faith increases and our understanding
broadens. In this process, our powers of reasoning will be

stretched to the limit, but we shall never again feel the need to use our brains in a faithless manner.

The appeal of the Scriptures to the believer's enlightened mind will remain strong to the end of his life. His interest in other things may wane but his delight in the Scriptures will not do so. Every time he opens his Bible, he is accepting the following invitation even though he is not conscious of it: '"Come now, let us reason together," says the LORD, "though your sins are like scarlet, they shall be as white as snow; though they are red as crimson, they shall be like wool"' (Isa. 1:18).

Let us then make good our inheritance and meditate more on God's precious word. Of course, there is an element of mystery about the gospel. Of course, we cannot fathom the way the Spirit works. Of course, it is important to believe when we cannot see. But when God speaks, he expects us to *think* about what he has said. God does not bypass the mind. Even at the moment faith is born in the human heart, the mind is fully involved. What did Jesus do when he appeared to the disciples after his resurrection? 'He opened their minds so they could understand the Scriptures' (Luke 24:45).

And what did the two disciples experience as Jesus talked to them on the road to Emmaus? Their hearts burned within them. Why? Because the Lord 'opened the Scriptures' to them (Luke 24:32). The burning hearts were the result of minds opening to the word of God. When this happens to us, we see the 'believe what you like' idea for what it is — an instrument of Satan to blind the godless. True faith will never give substance to fairies. Ideas that originate in the human mind will never set it free. The gods of our imagination cannot release us from the bondage of sin or give us hope in eternal life (John 8:32).

My own experience may be helpful. Before Christ drew me to himself, I was held back by a deep-seated reluctance to think deeply about anything. I tended to live for the moment and my mind was neither open nor free. In the main, ever-changing and usually corrupting ideas controlled it. I certainly did not submit to God's law, nor could I do so (Rom. 8:7).

At my conversion, so sudden and so sweeping was the change in this area that my friends were surprised. The next day I thought differently about almost everything. I was immediately aware of a keen desire to learn, particularly about God and the gospel. The desire has been growing ever since. Sixty-seven years on, the training and renewal of my mind is still a high priority. I have not the slightest doubt who has done this for me. It certainly wasn't the fairies.

8.

Saving faith is justifying

Therefore, since we have been justified through faith, we have peace with God through our Lord Jesus Christ, through whom we have gained access by faith into this grace in which we now stand. (Rom. 5:1-2)

Martin Luther

'Defender of the Faith' (*fidei defensor*) was a title given to the English monarch, Henry VIII, in 1521 by Pope Leo X. Oddly enough, it was awarded to him for writing a treatise against the teaching of Martin Luther (1483-1546). In spite of the fact that *fid def* or F.D. has appeared on British coins since the reign of George I, Luther was far better equipped to defend the faith than Henry. Luther's understanding of the faith was different from Henry's. The Holy Spirit through the Holy Scriptures had enlightened Luther's mind. The King's views were based on the 'faith' of the Roman Catholic Church.

The great reformer's anxiety about his own salvation and his failure to find peace with God through the rituals of the Roman Church caused him to abandon his regular duties in the monastery of the Augustinian Order. Finally, the Lord had mercy on him and opened his eyes to see that faith alone justifies a man before God. Luther describes his experience in these graphic words: 'The door of paradise was flung open to me and I entered'. The great man was wise enough to see that it was God himself who flung the door open. His unaided search for peace had failed miserably.

Luther's understanding of 'faith' now came into line with Scripture, carrying with it the meaning of personal trust in Christ. Evidence of Luther's transformed life was seen at once in his courageous public rejection of the errors of the Roman Church. In the light of God's word, transubstantiation (the teaching that the bread and wine in the Mass are changed into the actual body and blood of Christ), the mediatorial role of the priest, the doctrine of Purgatory, the Pope's claim to infallibility and the worship of the Virgin Mary were all rejected.

These errors had to go because Luther could not find them in the Bible and they conflicted with the basic doctrines of the Christian faith as he now understood them — God's righteousness, human sin, divine grace, the atonement and, not least, the doctrine of justification by faith. Indeed, the great reformer recognized the doctrine of justification as central to the gospel. For him, salvation through Christ alone was the same thing as justification through faith alone.

Justification is salvation

Although the doctrine has been constantly challenged, the Scriptures clearly teach that the sinner is saved at the moment when, by divine decree, his sins are put to Christ's account. And at the same moment, Christ's righteousness is put to the sinner's account (2 Cor. 5:21). God pronounces the believer 'not guilty'. He is saved from the terrible consequences of his sins and will not be condemned. There is no other way of being saved. The believer may not be able to say at what precise point in his life he was justified but, as we have said before, this is not important.

It is quite wrong, therefore, to suggest that Paul's doctrine of justification is not about how sinners are saved, as some scholars are now suggesting. Anyone who reads the Scriptures with an open mind will see at once that this is precisely what it is about. What can God's 'not guilty' verdict mean if it does not mean that I am saved from the consequences of my transgressions? Freedom from the condemnation of the law, which coincides with the divine verdict, can mean only one thing — I am now reconciled to God. Is this not what being saved is about?

It is possible, of course, that the sinner may be saved without hearing the word 'justification'. Even so, he has put his trust in Christ as his Substitute, the One who paid the penalty for his sins, and that is justification by faith. He should, however, quickly acquaint himself with the doctrine set out in Scripture.

In order to do this he is likely to be left to his own devices because the link between salvation and justification has been largely lost in the church today. There is a reluctance among ministers to preach about those unpleasant truths that make justification necessary — sin, guilt, condemnation, penal substitution and judgement. Many have taken it upon themselves to modify the message in the shameful and vain hope of making the gospel more appealing.

Although justification is salvation, the two words do not mean the same thing, just as in a human court the 'not guilty' verdict and the freedom that springs from it are not the same thing. The word 'salvation' covers the entire sweep of God's gracious provision for our lost condition. Justification on the other hand has to do with the legal status of those who trust in Christ. Nevertheless, it is impossible to be saved without being justified or to be justified without being saved.

Faith alone

Further, the faith that justifies stands alone. It is saving faith plus nothing. Those who are tempted to say, perhaps because of the teaching of James (to which we shall come later), that it is faith *and* deeds that justify should take careful note of Paul's words: 'For we maintain that a man is justified by faith apart from observing the law' (Rom. 3:28). Observing the law is our duty but it has nothing to do with our justification.

The words 'apart from observing the law' should not be misunderstood. We need to keep on emphasizing that such words do not mean that the justified man can break the law with impunity. The meaning is simple — our futile efforts to keep God's commandments contribute nothing to our justification. The contrast between what we have done and what Christ has done is very sharp and the choice is clear. If we trust in ourselves, we cannot trust in Christ. If we trust in Christ, we cannot trust in ourselves. To trust in the slightest degree in anything we have done is saying, in effect, that what Christ accomplished was not complete and, therefore, not sufficient to cover all our sins. A more grievous insult to our gracious God cannot be imagined.

Some are perplexed because heaven is sometimes spoken of as a reward. They cannot see how eternal life can be both a gift and a reward at the same time. Jesus said to his disciples: 'Blessed are you when people insult you, persecute you and falsely say all kinds of evil against you because of me. Rejoice and be glad, because great is your reward in heaven' (Matt. 5:11-12). It is obvious from other parts of Jesus' teaching that he is not saying that heaven is earned by what we do. He could not be more explicit on this point: 'I tell you the truth, whoever hears my word and believes him who sent me has eternal life and will not be condemned; he has crossed over from death to life' (John 5:24). Eternal life begins at the very moment the sinner is justified.

The problem vanishes altogether as soon as we understand that eternal life is spoken of as a recompense given by God to those who love him and honour him — that is to say, those who are justified by faith. Christians look forward with a sure and certain hope to their reward in heaven, which they could not do if it were in doubt. Rejoicing in our future reward is a sure indicator of living faith.

The Beatitudes of Jesus should be seen in this light. Take, for example, the words: 'Blessed are those who hunger and thirst for righteousness, for they will be filled' (Matt. 5:6). They will 'be filled' as a reward for their hungering and thirsting. But no one hungers and thirsts for righteousness unless he is in a right relationship with God. To put it another way, hunger after righteousness is one of the marks of the justified man, and his hunger will be fully satisfied.

Obviously, if just one single act of obedience to the law contributed to our justification, it would no longer be 'by faith alone'. To ponder Christ's summary of the commandments is a useful exercise for those who cling to the hope of being justified, even partially, by their deeds: '"Love the Lord your God with all your heart and with all your soul and with all your mind." This is the first and greatest commandment. And the second is like it: "Love your neighbour as yourself." All the Law and the Prophets hang on these two commandments.' (Matt. 22:37-40). Think about it. It is an impossible standard.

As believers, we have a duty and a desire to obey the law. But even if we live to be a hundred years old and serve the Lord faithfully, abstaining from every known sin, our title to eternal life will not be improved one bit. It cannot be. Obedience to the law is not a condition of our justification.

Justification by faith alone, then, is integral to the gospel. Forgiveness, reconciliation, grace, redemption and eternal life are all directly related to justifying faith. If we have not understood this, we need to start reading our Bibles. We are 'justified freely by his grace', says Paul, 'through the redemption

that came by Christ Jesus' (Rom. 3:24). 'God was reconciling
the world to himself in Christ, not counting men's sins against
them' (2 Cor. 5:19). God gave his Son to die 'so as to be just,
and the one who justifies those who have faith in Jesus'
(Rom. 3:26). 'Salvation is found in no-one else, for there is no
other name under heaven given to men by which we must be
saved' (Acts 4:12).

Those believers who, like Paul, are fully aware of the holiness of God and the wretchedness of their own sinful nature
(Rom. 7:24-25) have no difficulty in accepting the doctrine of
'faith alone'. They readily acknowledge their guilt before God
and their total indebtedness to the Lord Jesus Christ. Not
even the slightest suggestion of merit will escape their lips
because the power of the law to reach into their hearts and
expose their sins is part of their daily experience. They need
no persuading that 'no-one will be declared righteous in his
sight by observing the law; rather, through the law we become conscious of sin' (Rom. 3:20).

The psalmist felt this keenly: 'Out of the depths I cry to
you, O LORD; O Lord, hear my voice. Let your ears be
attentive to my cry for mercy. If you, O LORD, kept a record
of sins, O Lord, who could stand? But with you there is
forgiveness; therefore you are to be feared' (Ps. 130:1-4).

The beginning of a life of true holiness and righteousness
always involved the outright rejection of any other method of
being put right with God. We begin to serve God in perfect
freedom without a thought of earning merit. No more anxiety
about whether we are good enough, but only that inner
security that shows itself in faithful and dogged service for the
Master!

Clothed with Christ's righteousness

Here's a little puzzle for you. How can God be called righteous when he is not subject to any law? If righteousness is
defined as perfect obedience to God's law, can God be called
righteous on this basis? Not at all. The quality of righteousness is in God's nature and his law flows from his nature.
That is to say, God's law reveals his nature. The psalmist
understood this when he said: 'Righteous are you, O LORD,
and your laws are right' (Ps. 119:137). God's laws are righteous because God is righteous.

'But now', says Paul, 'a righteousness from God, apart
from law, has been made known, to which the Law and the
Prophets testify. This righteousness from God comes through
faith in Jesus Christ to all who believe' (Rom. 3:21-22). This
astonishing statement takes one's breath away. The perfect
righteousness of God is credited to me! Even to me! This is
something that never ceases to amaze me. A righteousness
that has nothing to do with my keeping the law is credited to
my account. One day soon, God's righteousness will be
imparted to me and then, this wretch will be like Jesus. He
will no longer be sheltering under his righteousness because it
will then be my own. The frustrated longing for perfection will
be fulfilled at last. What a glorious hope!

Vagrants were frequent callers at the Vicarage where I
lived. They came with their hard luck stories wanting money
which, judging by the smell of alcohol on the breath of some,
would be spent on more alcohol. Most were dirty, and some
very dirty. The scalp of one man I remember was so en-
crusted with dirt that I could have scraped it off.

Sometimes I felt like taking all their filthy clothes off and
putting them in the dustbin, and then putting the naked tramp
in a hot bath and giving him a good scrub. But what then? I
could not send him away naked, and it would have been

wrong to put his filthy garments back on. He would need new clothes as well.

So it is with the justified sinner. Even when his guilt, like filthy garments, has been removed and the defilement of sin washed away, he is still not in a fit state to be accepted by God. He needs new clothes. He needs to be covered with the righteousness of Christ.

9.

Father Abraham's faith

It was not through law that Abraham and his offspring received the promise that he would be heir of the world, but through the righteousness that comes by faith... Therefore, the promise comes by faith, so that it might be by grace and may be guaranteed to all Abraham's offspring.
(Rom. 4:13, 16)

Why read the Old Testament?

I received an e-mail from a relative in America. She wanted to know if my wife and I would visit the town of her childhood in Yorkshire and try to find out more about her family history. We made the journey and decided to start our enquiries at the local chemist's shop. 'I am not your man', said the chemist, 'but I know the very man you want. What he doesn't know about the history of this town is not worth knowing.'

We located the little cottage where the man lived and eagerly knocked on the door. An elderly, but sprightly, gentleman appeared and I explained to him why we had come. 'Oh no', he replied, 'I am not into that sort of thing. I live for the future.' I do not think the chemist was mistaken. It was just that the old man did not want to *talk* about the past.

He invited us in and we chatted for a while on various subjects and I was agreeably surprised that a person of his age
was so forward looking. I could not help thinking about the
people I have known who, as they grew older, lived more and
more in the past and found it hard to relate to the modern
world. Not this man!

Nevertheless, I was not happy with his decision to ignore
all his memory links with the past. History had obviously
become a bore to him. I remembered my school days when I
took a similar view of history, by default in my case, rather
than choice. Yet, after my conversion, my attitude changed
completely. History fascinated me and the more I learned
about the past, the better I understood the present.

A similar thing happened when I applied my mind to the
history of the Old Testament. What I once regarded as
extraneous and uninteresting became alive and relevant. I
discovered that the knowledge of what happened in the Old is
the key to understanding the New and, in some ways, to
understanding the situation in the church of today.

Getting to grips with the doctrine of justification by faith
was no exception to this general rule. I discovered that what
God had done for me, he had also done for Abraham way
back in the Book of Genesis. Because of my conversion to
Christ, I had become one of Abraham's children and an
inheritor of the promises God made to him!

The problem we have today is that a high percentage of
believers fail to realize this because they, too, are not very
interested in Old Testament history. The probability is that if
such people are reading this book, they will be tempted to
skip this chapter because it is all about Abraham who lived a
very long time ago. If they do, they will be the losers.

For the study of justification by faith, a thorough understanding of the role of Abraham in the history of redemption
is essential. It can even be life-transforming. God's dealings
with Abraham will teach us that far from being God's new
idea, justification by faith predates the giving of the law to

Moses by four and a half centuries. The Law of Moses was not, as some think, a new departure, but a logical development of the covenant established with Abraham. The purpose of the commandments God gave to Moses is to expose sin and highlight the need for the gospel (Rom. 3:20). In other words, careful reading of the Old Testament will teach us that God did not have several plans for the redemption of his people, but just one.

If we may digress for a moment, the people known as dispensationalists believe that God had a different purpose for each period, or each dispensation. The time before the fall of Adam is regarded as the dispensation of innocence, from Adam to Noah, the dispensation of conscience, from Abraham to Moses the dispensation of promise and so on. Most dispensationalists think there are seven of these periods.

Although they tend to deny it, dispensationalists teach that God's way of salvation changed over these periods. For example, they say that salvation in the Old Testament was not through faith in Christ. What then did the apostle Peter mean when he said that 'Salvation is found in no-one else, for there is no other name under heaven given to men by which we must be saved' (Acts 4:12)? True, the believers in the Old Testament did not know as much about the Lord Jesus Christ as we do. Nor did they know his Name, but it was through him that they were justified. His death covers the sins of all his people, no matter when they lived.

In particular, dispensationalists regard the covenant with Abraham as a Jewish covenant. Therefore, they say, it has no direct link with the New Covenant. Yet, it is obvious from Paul's teaching that Abraham was justified by faith in Christ. We should not be deceived — the gospel was, is, and always will be the only way to heaven. As Paul says, God 'announced the gospel in advance to Abraham' (Gal. 3:8).

Who is Abraham?

A lot of fantasy surrounds the person of Abraham, not least because of the Islamic legends that survive about him. According to these, Abraham was not the son of Terah as the Bible says, but of a certain Prince Azar and his wife Adna. At the age of eighteen months, he had developed into a very wise boy who seemed to be about fifteen years old. Perhaps this was because he sucked two of his mother's fingers, one of which yielded milk and the other honey!

The Abraham we are talking about, however, was a real man who lived somewhere around 1900BC. He was indeed wise, but not by sucking his mother's fingers. He was, and still is, a very important person, more important than most Christians realize. The Scriptures will not allow us to ignore the man who became God's friend (2 Chr. 20:7). Indeed, God was pleased to reveal himself as 'the God of Abraham, the God of Isaac and the God of Jacob' (Exod. 3:15).

Abraham (formerly Abram) was born in Ur, a city probably located in what is now Iraq. He was married to Sarai (who became Sarah) and lived with his father Terah and his two brothers Nahor and Haran. God called him to leave his country and his father's household, and go to a land that God would show him (Gen. 12:1). The writer to the Hebrews tells us that Abraham 'obeyed and went, even though he did not know where he was going' (Heb. 11:8).

It seems that Abraham's father Terah did not share his son's faith. As far as Terah was concerned, the move from Ur was no more than an astute change of location, probably because of the threat of war. So 'Terah took his son Abram, his grandson Lot son of Haran, and his daughter-in-law Sarai, the wife of his son Abram, and together they set out from Ur of the Chaldeans to go to Canaan. But when they came to Haran, they settled there' (Gen. 11:31). The journey from Ur to Haran is about six hundred miles to the northwest.

When he was seventy-five years of age, and after his father had died in Haran, Abraham left with his wife and his nephew Lot, together with the possessions and the people they had acquired in Haran, to go to Canaan (Gen. 12:4-5). The long journey that followed is remarkable.

More remarkable, however, were the promises God made to Abraham. They are so far-reaching it is not easy to grasp their full significance. They give us the clue to the meaning of the history and destiny of the world and the church and are, therefore, important for every Christian believer: 'I will make you into a great nation and I will bless you; I will make your name great, and you will be a blessing. I will bless those who bless you, and whoever curses you I will curse; and all peoples on earth will be blessed through you' (Gen. 12:2-3). On his arrival in Canaan, God appeared to him and said, 'To your offspring I will give this land' (Gen. 12:7).

Having no children, Abraham adopted one of his servants as his heir (Gen. 15:2-3). But God appeared to him in a vision and said: '"This man will not be your heir, but a son coming from your own body will be your heir." He took him outside and said, "Look up at the heavens and count the stars — if indeed you can count them." Then he said to him, "So shall your offspring be"' (Gen. 15:4-5). This promise is amazing. As we shall see, it is fulfilled, not in the natural children of Abraham, as may at first be supposed, but in the innumerable company of believers who lived before and after Christ, Jew or Gentile — Gentile being the name the Bible uses for all non-Jews.

God did not befriend Abraham because he was special in some way. Although a man of great faith, there were many blemishes in his character. He deceived Pharaoh, king of Egypt, by saying that his wife Sarah was his sister. Abraham was afraid that since Sarah was a beautiful woman, the Egyptians might kill him and take her (Gen. 12:11-13). He failed in the same way with Abimelech, king of Gerar (Gen. 20). There was some truth in Abraham's claim that

Sarah was his sister because she was the daughter of his father but not his mother (Gen. 20:12). It was deception nevertheless.

Even worse was Abraham's failure to wait for God to fulfil his promise of a son. He gave in to the faithless suggestion of his wife, Sarah, that he should sleep with Hagar, her Egyptian servant (Gen. 16:1-2). Hagar conceived and gave birth to Ishmael, but nothing but misery ensued. Indeed, Hagar now stands as a warning to all who think they can gain God's favour by self-effort (Gal. 4:25). The fulfilment of God's promise would come in God's way and in God's time and neither Abraham nor Sarah could do anything to hurry it up. When it came, it would be a miracle because both Abraham and Sarah would be far too old to have children (Rom. 4:19-22).

A further thirteen years elapsed. Had God forgotten? Then one day the Lord appeared to Abraham again and gave him the thrilling news: 'I will surely return to you about this time next year, and Sarah your wife will have a son' (Gen. 18:10). Sarah, who was listening, laughed to herself because, being very old, the promise seemed too ridiculous for words. 'Then the LORD said to Abraham, "Why did Sarah laugh and say, 'Will I really have a child, now that I am old?' Is anything too hard for the LORD?"' (Gen. 18:13-14).

The long wait was finally ended when 'the LORD was gracious to Sarah as he had said, and the LORD did for Sarah what he had promised. Sarah became pregnant and bore a son to Abraham in his old age, at the very time God had promised him. Abraham gave the name Isaac to the son Sarah bore him' (Gen. 21:1-3).

Further tests of Abraham's faith were yet to come. The fiercest came when God called him to sacrifice the promised son, Isaac, for whom he had waited so long. This time he came through the test with flying colours because by now 'Abraham reasoned that God could raise the dead, and figuratively speaking, he did receive Isaac back from death'

(Heb. 11:19). God provided a ram for the sacrifice instead
(Gen. 22:1-18).

Why is he important?

We must not think that natural descent from Abraham
brought no advantages for the Jews. Their squandered
privileges made their rejection painful for Paul. Being a Jew
himself, he experienced 'great sorrow and unceasing anguish'
in his heart (Rom. 9:2). 'For I could wish that I myself were
cursed and cut off from Christ for the sake of my brothers,
those of my own race, the people of Israel. Theirs is the
adoption as sons; theirs the divine glory, the covenants, the
receiving of the law, the temple worship and the promises.
Theirs are the patriarchs, and from them is traced the human
ancestry of Christ, who is God over all, for ever praised!
Amen' (Rom. 9:3-5).

Later on in his letter to the Romans, the apostle tells us
that God has not completely rejected the Jews. They did not
'stumble so as to fall beyond recovery' (Rom. 11:1,11). God
was not mistaken in choosing Israel. Nor has his purpose
been overthrown by the Jews' disobedience. It was never
God's intention to confine the blessings promised to Abraham
to the Jews only. They were intended for Gentiles too
(Rom. 11:25-26).

Qualification to receive these blessings, therefore, has
nothing to do with nationality. It has everything to do with
being born of the Spirit into God's family, which includes
people from every nation (Rev. 7:9). Paul puts it in these
words: 'It is not as though God's word had failed. For not all
who are descended from Israel are Israel. Nor because they
are his descendents are they all Abraham's children. On the
contrary, "It is through Isaac that your offspring will be
reckoned." In other words, it is not the natural children who

are God's children, but it is the children of the promise who are regarded as Abraham's offspring' (Rom. 9:6-8).

For those who may find this difficult, let me try to fill it out a bit. Just because many natural children of Jacob were faithless, and, therefore, do not belong to the true Israel, it does not mean that God has failed to keep his promise to Abraham. The true Israel of God is the true church of Christ. It consists of people who, like Abraham, believe God's promises.

Isaac was indeed a miracle baby, born as a direct result of God's promise. Therefore, all who follow the example of Abraham and trust in God's word are 'children of the promise' and therefore Abraham's true children. This is what God meant when he told Abraham: 'It is through Isaac that your offspring will be reckoned' (Gen. 21:12).

This is in harmony with the words of Paul in Gal. 3:29: 'If you belong to Christ, then you are Abraham's seed, and heirs according to the promise'. Therefore, since God is now my Father, Abraham is my father. As John Stott says, 'We take our place in the noble historic succession of faith' (*The Message of Galatians*, Inter Varsity Press, p.101).

The name 'Covenant of Grace' is given to the agreement God imposed on Abraham. The word 'grace' means 'unmerited favour' and the promises that reveal God's grace to all his people are enshrined in that covenant. In particular, the pledge that 'all the peoples of the earth' would be blessed through Abraham (Gen. 12:3). The covenant promises are universal in their application. This does not mean, however, that the Covenant of Grace is made with 'every living creature' as was the case with the covenant with Noah (Gen. 9:12). But it certainly means that the promises extend to believers of every age and every nation.

It should now be obvious why Abraham is so important. In many ways, ignorance about him is a sad outcome of the continuing belief that the Old Testament is all about law, and the New all about grace. Many still think of Abraham as the father of the Jews, but that is as far as it goes. Even worse, they think that all the promises God made to Abraham were temporal — to do with the land of Canaan and nothing more.

Why is he our father?

Founding Fathers are men whose names are remembered because they established institutions that have stood the test of time. For example, the politicians who signed the Declaration of Independence are known as the Founding Fathers of the United States. In a very real sense, Abraham is not only the founding father of the Jewish nation, but also of the Christian Church.

We have already noted Paul's assertion that it is not Abraham's natural children who are God's children. In Romans chapter four he explains this in more detail. Some may find his argument hard to follow, but it is well worth persevering. Speaking about the blessedness of the man 'whose sin the Lord will never count against him' he poses the question: 'Is this blessedness only for the circumcised [the Jews], or also for the uncircumcised?' (verses 8-9). He goes on to explain that Abraham 'received the sign of circumcision, a seal of the righteousness that he had by faith while he was still uncircumcised' (verse 11). In other words, he was not justified because he was circumcised, but because he believed.

Circumcision, the seal of the righteousness of God that was now credited to Abraham's account, came later. Since circumcision was an outward sign or seal of Abraham's faith, it could not be the cause of it. The Jews made the mistake of thinking they were right with God *because* they had been circumcised. Many church folk make the same mistake with regard to baptism.

Therefore, says the apostle, Abraham 'is the father of all who believe but have not been circumcised [Gentiles], in order that righteousness may be credited to them. And he is also the father of the circumcised [Jews] who are not only circumcised but who also walk in the footsteps of the faith that our father Abraham had before he was circumcised' (verses 11-12). In short, he is the father of all who are justified by faith.

We may also regard Abraham as our father because we are accepted by God on the same basis as he was. When God promised him that his offspring would be as numerous as the stars, we are told that 'Abram believed the LORD, and he credited it to him as righteousness' (Gen. 15:6). On the basis of their trust in God to fulfil his promises, righteousness is still credited to all who believe, and they too receive all the blessings enshrined in the promises to Abraham. As it was with Abraham, so it is with us.

As we know, many of Abraham's descendants with whom the covenant was established forfeited its blessings by their disobedience. Because of this, some conclude that God's election is not a matter of being chosen for eternal life but merely for privilege. That is to say, the Jews were better placed to believe than anyone else. But how can this be true if God chose us in Christ 'before the creation of the world' and 'predestined us to be adopted as his sons through Jesus Christ, in accordance with his pleasure and will' (Eph. 1:4-5)?

The separation between the elect and reprobate Jews is seen clearly in the fulfilment of God's promise to Abraham. It was a separation between those who inherited the promised blessing and those who did not. Since it is the children of the promise who are Abraham's true children, it follows that the elect are those people who have the same kind of trust in God's promises that Abraham did.

The Jews, the natural descendents of Abraham, were convinced that they only were members of the covenant made with Abraham and that all the promises applied to them and no one else. After all, they had received the sign of circumcision! Yet only a remnant, chosen by grace, were saved (Rom. 11:5); the rest were not the children of God because they were not the 'children of the promise'.

Paul sheds more light on the problem in the following words: 'A man is not a Jew if he is only one outwardly, nor is circumcision merely outward and physical. No, a man is a Jew if he is one inwardly; and circumcision is circumcision of the heart, by the Spirit, not by the written code (Rom. 2:28-29).

The covenant stands

Just recently, my wife and I made a new will. Over the years, our circumstances have changed a lot. Our 'children' are grown up and have grown up 'children' of their own, so a new will became necessary. Between now and the day we die, we are the only ones who can make changes to our wills. After that, we cannot make changes either. The promises made in our wills will then become permanent.

The writer to the Hebrews makes the same point: 'In the case of a will, it is necessary to prove the death of the one who made it, because a will is only in force when somebody has died; it never takes effect while the one who made it is living' (Heb. 9:16-17). Careful reading of the passage will show that the writer is saying that the death of Christ was necessary in order to make the covenant with Abraham effective. 'Christ is the mediator of a new covenant, that those who are called may receive the promised eternal inheritance' (Heb. 9:15).

Paul, too, says the same thing in different words in Galatians 3:15: 'Just as no-one can set aside or add to a human covenant that has been duly established, so it is in this case'.

God made a will — a covenant — in which he made promises to Abraham, a will that cannot be changed. It is an everlasting covenant.

The promises, therefore, cannot be anything other than spiritual. Even the promise of territory in the land of Canaan, at its root, was spiritual, as Abraham himself realized. He was not looking forward to inheriting a strip of land on this earth, but 'to the city with foundations, whose architect and builder is God' (Heb. 11:10).

Although God was at work redeeming his people from the time of Adam, the reader should realize that the astonishing call of Abraham and the covenant God established with him, really mark the beginning of the history of redemption. We have already seen that along with the pledge that Abraham would have a son and heir came the promise that he would be the father of many nations (Gen. 17:5) and that it would not be possible to count his offspring. To suggest that this was fulfilled in the emergence of the Midianite (Gen. 25:2), Ishmaelite (Gen. 25:12), and Edomite (Gen. 36:31) nations, robs the promise of its meaning.

Biblical illiteracy is the main reason why the importance of Abraham is not recognized. In their ignorance, many believers still work on that absurd principle mentioned earlier, that the Old Testament is all about law and the New all about grace. They see the New Testament as a kind of emergency rescue plan because keeping the Old Testament law as a means of going to heaven did not work. This is no insignificant mistake. Their spiritual lives are impoverished as a result.

A warning

The Jews were proud of their descent from Abraham. They believed that they were the ones to whom the promised blessings would come. They were seriously mistaken. Their sense of security was false. 'If you were Abraham's children' Jesus said, 'then you would do the things Abraham did. As it is, you are determined to kill me...' (John 8:39-40). 'You belong to your father, the devil, and you want to carry out your father's desire' (John 8:44).

This leaves us with a very important question that concerns all of us. Why did so many of Abraham's natural descendants not inherit the blessing? Why did they not believe? Why were they not justified by faith? Some would say it is because they were not chosen for eternal life. But this will not do. Although we may have difficulty coping with the apparent tension between election and human responsibility, we cannot shift the blame to God. The gospel is a genuine offer of forgiveness and God has promised to receive all who will repent and believe. If, like the Jews, we are privileged to have access to the counsels of God, we must use them to the full.

The unbelieving Jews were rejected because they tried to establish their own righteousness instead of repenting and accepting God's righteousness. They 'pursued a law of righteousness' but they did not pursue it 'by faith but as if it were by works. They stumbled over the "stumbling stone". As it is written: "See I lay in Zion a stone that causes men to stumble and a rock that makes them fall, and the one who trusts in him will never be put to shame"' (Rom. 9:31-33). Let us be sure that we do not make the same mistake.

Do we believe then, as Abraham did, that nothing is too hard for the Lord? Do we readily accept that, like Abraham, we are sinners — whether we know God's law or not? Do we believe that the blessings God bestowed on Abraham were by faith alone and that we can do nothing to deserve them? If we can answer 'Yes' to these questions we may regard ourselves as the true children of Abraham. We are 'Blessed along with Abraham, the man of faith' (Gal. 3:9).

Jesus said: 'I say to you that many will come from the east and the west, and will take their places at the feast with

Abraham, Isaac and Jacob in the kingdom of heaven. But the subjects of the kingdom will be thrown outside, into the darkness, where there will be weeping and gnashing of teeth' (Matt. 8:11-12). So near, yet so far.

10.

False faith

Yet they lean upon the LORD and say, 'Is not the LORD among us? No disaster will come upon us.' (Micah 3:11)

Temporary faith

If we can imagine a fearless prophet denouncing the Prime Minister and the Archbishop of Canterbury (Primate of all England and senior bishop in the worldwide Anglican Communion) both at the same time, we shall have some idea what it was like in Israel when the prophet Micah rebuked the leaders of the nation. Among the charges laid against them was the sin of presumption. They believed God was among them and would deliver them from disaster. But their faith was false and their security illusory.

Many people today are guilty of the same sin. They want God on their side but they neither glorify him as God, nor give thanks to him (Rom. 1:21). Some will call upon him when they are in trouble and do not know where to turn, but they revert to their godless lifestyle as soon as the crisis passes.

I was called to see a man whose young wife had just died. Through his tears, he told me how she had collapsed in his arms the previous evening as they were dancing together. He was inconsolable. After the funeral, I visited him and he told me he was anxious to talk to me about 'religion'. He felt that he had been living for work and pleasure without a thought of God, but now he was determined to change. We talked at some length and I invited him to come to church.

After coming every Sunday for a few weeks, he began to miss. A few weeks later, he stopped coming altogether and I went round to see him again. He was no longer interested. Oh yes, he believed in God, but coming to church had been an emotional reaction to his bereavement. He was now back to normal, and felt no further need of the church or its vicar!

This has been called transitory or temporary faith. Although the man in this case was right to think of putting God first in his life after the tragedy, there was no permanent change in his heart. As the pain of his loss eased, his resolve began to weaken. His 'faith' was temporary.

During the Second World War, I was a radio operator. My job was to listen to transmissions by our own units and to note any breaches of security. We always worked on the principle that the enemy was listening. When tuning to a particular station I had to be aware of what we called the 'harmonic frequency' — a kind of overtone or echo of the true frequency. To all intents and purposes, it sounded just like the real thing.

What is good always has its counterfeits, and faith is no exception. Sometimes the counterfeits are so good that it is hard to distinguish them from the real thing, especially to the inexperienced eye. I recall speaking to a women's group on this subject and, during the talk, I passed round two rings. One had a large imitation 'stone' ('paste' to those who are familiar with the subject) and the other, three smaller brilliant cut diamonds. I asked the women if they could tell me which of the rings was genuine. Of about twenty women, some thought they were both genuine and others thought both were a good imitation.

It can sometimes be just as difficult to the inexperienced observer to distinguish between true faith and temporary faith. One young teenager in particular comes to mind. After he professed faith in Christ, there were clear signs of a change. He had a remarkable understanding of the Scriptures, he stopped using bad language and he was eager to share his faith with others. But like Demas (2 Tim. 4:10), he loved this world and within a year, he deserted the church and the Lord as well. Now, I am not easily taken in. Indeed, more than once I have been accused of tardiness in recognizing that someone has become a true believer. Yet, this young man convinced me.

All this is in harmony with the Scriptures. Jesus himself warned us about it in the parable of the sower (Matt. 13:3-9; 18-23). A farmer went out to sow his seed. Some fell along the path, and the birds came and ate it up. Some fell on rocky places and sprang up quickly, but because the soil was shallow, it had no root and was scorched by the sun. Other seed fell among thorns, which grew up and choked the seed. Still other seed fell on good soil, where it produced a crop — a hundred, sixty or thirty times what was sown.

Jesus explains the meaning of the parable. The seed is the word of God. The seed on the path represents those who hear the gospel but do not understand it. The evil one snatches the seed away so that it bears no fruit. The seed on the stony ground is the person who hears the gospel with joy but has no root. When trouble or persecution comes, he quickly falls away. He does not bear fruit either.

The thorny ground is like the person who is serious about his faith, but the worries of life and the deceitfulness of wealth choke the seed. It too, is unfruitful. The person who hears the gospel and understands it, is like the seed on the good soil. He produces a crop. The size of the crop will vary, but the line between those who are saved and those who are lost must be drawn between the fruit-bearing seed and the rest.

The young man mentioned above was like the seed that fell on rocky places where it did not have much soil. He received the word with joy but, since he had no root, he lasted only a short time. But others, like the seed on the thorny ground, may last much longer. Eventually, however, they too are distracted by the world or deceived by the love of money, and fall away.

Hebrews 6:4-6 is very important in this connexion. It shows to what extent temporary faith can develop. The writer speaks of those who 'have once been enlightened, who have tasted the heavenly gift, who have shared in the Holy Spirit, who have tasted the goodness of the word of God and the powers of the coming age'. Many Christians find it hard to accept that this describes those who were never truly saved, but this is clearly the case.

The writer himself implies that the people who were 'enlightened' and who 'shared in the Holy Spirit', and 'tasted the goodness of the word of God' did not have true faith. At verse nine he says that he is 'confident of better things' in those to whom he writes, 'things that accompany salvation'. It is possible, therefore, to have all these blessings and yet not have the things that accompany salvation — in other words, to remain unsaved.

We need to remember what Jesus said to those who prophesied, drove out demons and performed many miracles in his name — 'I never knew you. Away from me, you evildoers!' (Matt. 7:22-23).

Formal faith

Who were the people who plotted to arrest Jesus and kill him? 'Then the chief priest and the elders of the people assembled in the palace of the high priest, whose name was Caiaphas, and they plotted to arrest Jesus in some sly way and kill him' (Matt. 26:3-4). Was it not Cardinal Wolsey who publicly burnt the books of the great reformer Martin Luther in St Paul's Cathedral, in the presence of bishops and other church dignitaries? The Bible tells us that Christ's enemies were religious formalists.

It was at an ecclesiastical court that William Tyndale was accused of having infringed the imperial decree which forbade the teaching of justification by faith alone. It was with the consent of the church that the outstanding Bible translator was strangled and burned. So we could go on to talk about Archbishop Cranmer, bishops Latimer and Ridley, and a host of other fine Christian men and women who were hounded to death by so-called churchmen.

The same is true in my own experience. The people who are first to persecute young converts are church people — people who, in spite of their profession know nothing of a vital, life-transforming faith in Christ. It is a rare thing in the Church of England these days for a man who loves and preaches the gospel to have the whole-hearted support of his bishop.

To the Pharisees, Jesus said: 'Isaiah was right when he prophesied about you hypocrites; as it is written: "These people honour me with their lips, but their hearts are far from me. They worship me in vain; their teachings are but rules taught by men"' (Mark 7:6-7). Two thousand years have passed since Jesus uttered these words and yet, the problem is still with us. I have lost count of the number of church people I have known who would fight to the last drop of blood to preserve out-dated traditions, and yet thought nothing of Christ.

In his defence before the governor Felix, Paul gives us an interesting insight into this problem: 'I admit that I worship the God of our fathers as a follower of the Way, which they call a sect. I believe everything that agrees with the Law and that is written in the Prophets, and I have the same hope in God as

these men, that there will be a resurrection of both the righteous and the wicked' (Acts 24:14-15).

Paul's purpose here is to prove that he was not a sectarian.
His faith (what he believed) was not some new-fangled
doctrine. It was no different from that of the men who were
bringing charges against him. Indeed, it was the 'faith' of all
Israelites. But just because he took his religion seriously, he
was accused of sectarianism. An angry clergyman once
accused me of sectarianism just because, like Paul, I took the
Scriptures seriously.

So, what was the difference? The vital ingredient in Paul's
case was that he trusted Christ personally and completely.
With him, it was not a matter of perpetuating tradition but of
having a living relationship with God. How many times, I
wonder, have those who truly believe 'the faith that was once
for all entrusted to the saints' (Jude 3) been accused of
departing from it? This is how it often seems to the formalists
because the difference between their lifeless traditions and the
living faith of true believers is so great. Indeed, it is possible to
be a member of many churches today and never see vital
Christianity in action.

Vain faith

'By this gospel you are saved,' says Paul, 'if you hold firmly to
the word I preached to you. Otherwise, you have believed in
vain' (1 Cor. 15:2). What was the word he preached to them?
He goes on to tell us: 'For what I received I passed on to you
as of first importance: that Christ died for our sins according
to the Scriptures, that he was buried, that he was raised on
the third day according to the Scriptures...' (verses 3-4).

The apostle's meaning is unmistakeable. If the Corinthians
do not believe in the resurrection of Jesus Christ, their faith is
worthless. The warning is just as necessary today as it was so

long ago. To embrace the gospel Paul preached brings salvation. The Corinthian edited version does not. Yet, so many people today, who would call themselves believers, deny the bodily resurrection of Christ and vainly hope they will go to heaven.

I have vague memories of my teddy bear. It fell to pieces because of the rough handling I gave it. First, one of its ears came off and then, I think, one of its arms. Both its eyes came out as well as a result of being pulled by destructive fingers. Eventually it split at the seams and was disembowelled. My memory tells me that it was stuffed with straw, but I cannot be sure. What I can be sure about is that it became a shadow of its former self and was hardly recognizable as a teddy bear.

God's way of salvation, as Paul proclaimed it, suffers in the same way at the hands of wicked preachers. On their own authority, they remove the bits they do not like and end up with a pathetic message emptied of all meaning. They take it upon themselves to determine what is appropriate for today, and what is not.

'Do men make their own gods?' asks Jeremiah. 'Yes, but they are not gods!' (Jer. 16:20). How can anyone be such a fool as to put his trust in something coming out of the dark recesses of his biased mind? Let us beware. Christian orthodoxy can quickly degenerate into idolatry. Christian worship can easily become a cover for the worship of false gods. Once the authority of the Scriptures is rejected, there is no limit to the destructive manipulation of God and his gospel.

The same is true of the character of Christ. To deny his deity or refuse to believe he is fully God and fully man, will certainly bar the way to eternal life. If we do this, we are no better than Jehovah's Witnesses who, against all the textual evidence, make a special point of calling him 'a god' (John 1:1, New World Translation). That John, a Hebrew monotheist, to whom the idea of another god would be abhorrent, could introduce such an idea into his Gospel is too ridiculous for words.

By reading the Scriptures, every believer should be constantly improving his knowledge of God, but inadequate understanding is not the same as denial. Gaps in our knowledge do not make our faith false. Denial of revealed truth, however, is a very different matter. 'Faith' in a 'god' whose sovereignty is denied, for example, is false because such a god does not exist. As soon as we begin to feel free to strip the God of Israel of everything we do not like about him, we are making shipwreck of our faith (1 Tim. 1:19). We end up believing in a god who is a figment of our imagination.

Since God searches the heart, he knows precisely what kind of faith we have. When people saw the miracles Jesus performed, many '...believed in his name. But Jesus would not entrust himself to them, for he knew all men' (John 2:23-24). On this passage, Bishop Ryle says: 'There is a faith which devils have, and a faith which is the gift of God. The persons mentioned in this verse had the former, but not the latter' (*Expository Thoughts on the Gospels*, James Clarke and Company).

Inherited faith

If anyone had good reason in the eyes of others to boast about his pedigree, it was the apostle Paul: 'If anyone else thinks he has reasons to put confidence in the flesh, I have more: circumcised on the eighth day, of the people of Israel, of the tribe of Benjamin, a Hebrew of the Hebrews; in regard to the law, a Pharisee; as for zeal, persecuting the church; as for legalistic righteousness, faultless' (Phil. 3:4-6).

What privileges! He was a true Jew, a direct descendant of Abraham. His parents brought him up in strict accordance with the law. He says: 'I was advancing in Judaism beyond many Jews of my own age, and was extremely zealous for the traditions of my fathers' (Gal. 1:14). He had chosen to become a Pharisee and persecuted the church with utmost zeal because he believed the Christians were worshipping another god. If judged by his external observance of the law, he was blameless.

The apostle was not motivated by jealousy either. He did not deride such privileges because he did not have them. On the contrary, no one was more privileged than he. But he did not trust in these advantages because he knew that they had no merit whatever in the matter of justification before God.

This inherited faith is still with us. Many church people are proud of their pedigree. They were born into good religious families, accepted into the church, taught to say their prayers and live morally upright lives. They consent to the teaching of the church. Like Paul, they regard these things as good. But unlike Paul, they make the serious mistake of thinking that these benefits are sufficient to qualify them to go to heaven.

It is, of course, vitally important to teach our children about the faith. It is good for them to follow the example of their parents in this matter. But there must come a time when their faith becomes their own — when they themselves put their trust in Christ. This is what happened in the case of Timothy, so that Paul was able to say to him: 'I have been reminded of your sincere faith, which first lived in your grandmother Lois and in your mother Eunice and, I am persuaded, now lives in you also' (2 Tim. 1:5).

If, however, the faith passed down is only in the mind and finds expression merely in external forms and ceremonies, it is perpetrating a tradition and nothing more. Such 'faith' often blinds a person to his need of Christ. It encourages him to think that conversion is something only outsiders need. It does not produce a genuine love for the word of God or the people of God. Indeed, many with this kind of faith react strongly to the suggestion that their status and their long membership of the church have no value as far as their salvation is concerned.

The remedy

How refreshing it is to turn from this depressing scene and hear Jesus saying to the Sadducees: 'You are in error because you do not know the Scriptures or the power of God' (Matt. 22:29). At first sight, it appears the Sadducees were ignorant of *two* things — the Scriptures and the power of God — but this is not the case. Their ignorance of the Scriptures was their basic problem and that led inevitably to ignorance of God's power, and many other things as well. In fact, the Sadducees did have some knowledge of the Scriptures but like so many people today, they did not get the message.

Let us be warned. It is fearfully possible to have some knowledge of the Scriptures and still be ignorant of God's power. Let us be wary lest we fail to recognize the seriousness of wilfully closing the mind against the truth of Scripture. Jesus taught in parables so that those who, by the mercy of God, were willing to be taught might understand. For others, however, the prophecy of Isaiah was fulfilled: 'You will be ever hearing but never understanding; you will be ever seeing but never perceiving' (Matt. 13:14).

The cure for false faith, then, is to come back to the Bible and open our hearts to its precious truth. We need to pray as earnestly as we know how, that the Lord will have mercy on us. We need to plead with him to open our blind eyes to see the one who is 'the way and the truth and the life'. No-one comes to the Father except through him (John 14:6). He is the only Saviour; he is also the man whom God has appointed to judge the world with justice (Acts 17:31). As the Irishman said, 'On Christ the solid rock I stand, all other rocks are sham rocks.' (For readers who may not know, the shamrock is a plant that is the national emblem of Ireland.)

11.

Dead faith

You see that a person is justified by what he does and not by faith alone. (James 2:24)

What question is James answering?

A man woke up in the small hours of the morning and immediately detected the smell of burning. He jumped out of bed and opened the bedroom door only to be confronted by flames leaping up the staircase. He quickly roused his wife and children and arranged for her to drop the children from the bedroom window. He would go first and catch them from below. The man dropped into the street from the window and waited, but no faces appeared at the window. His wife and children had been overwhelmed by the fire and perished.

At least, this was the man's story when he appeared in court. Since I was only a child at the time, I cannot remember whether he was charged with manslaughter or murder. Either way, he was found not guilty. There was no evidence to prove the charge against him. But the majority of the population of the town were not convinced of his innocence and the poor man was left in no doubt how they felt. I have a vivid memory of seeing him walking furtively down the street with his coat collar and hat combining to cover his face.

Here was a man who was innocent in the eyes of the law but not in almost everyone else's. He could not justify his claim to be innocent in the eyes of the people because his behaviour appeared to suggest otherwise. I suppose if he had put his wife out first to catch the children, there would have been no problem.

The apostle James writes about people who claim to be justified in the eyes of God but who cannot justify their claim in the eyes of the people. Therefore, when James concludes that 'a person is justified by what he does and not by faith alone' (James 2:24), he is, in effect, saying that righteous and compassionate living is the only justification for anyone's claim to be right with God. Those who assume that James is contradicting Paul fail to see this.

Let us go back to the man who lost his wife and family in the house fire. If we pose the question: 'Was he justified or not?' it is impossible to answer until we know what the question means. If it means, 'Was he justified before the law?' the answer is 'Yes'. But if it means, 'Was he justified before the people?' the answer is 'No'. There is no contradiction because the question is different.

James, therefore, is not contradicting Paul because they are answering different questions. Paul is answering the question: 'How may a man be justified before God? The answer is 'By faith in Christ'. James is answering the question: 'How is a justified man justified before the people?' The answer is 'By living a holy and righteous life'.

Those who want to be contentious will not see it this way. Some go so far as to suggest that since the letter of James was written later, he understood the weakness in Paul's argument and, therefore, he must be seen as Paul's interpreter. Such ideas will only create yet more confusion over a doctrine that is as clear as daylight.

On the other hand, believers who have no axe to grind and are concerned only to seek the truth, will see that James is not supplementing Paul, but protecting the doctrine of justification by faith from those who want to use it as a basis for sin. As we saw earlier, these people are called antinomians (people who believe that 'Christians are released by grace from obeying moral laws' [*Oxford English Dictionary*]).

Antinomians assume that because they believe it in their minds, they can go on living like unbelievers. They are guilty of using the grace of God as an excuse for continuing in sin.

What does James mean by 'justification'?

James is using the word 'justified' in a different sense. Paul is using the word in a legal sense. He is talking about God's 'not guilty' verdict on the believing sinner. James uses the word in the sense of 'making good one's claim before a watching world'. Is his claim to be right with God justified in the eyes of others?

James's statement that 'a person is justified by what he does and not by faith alone' (James 2:24) must be seen in this light. Once we realize that the word 'justification' is being used in a different way from Paul, the supposed contradiction between the two apostles disappears. When Paul uses the word, he is talking about justification before God.

In fact, if anyone's claim to be justified before God did not lead to sanctification, Paul was just as determined as James to reject it. We sense Paul's alarm in his writings: 'What shall we say, then? Shall we go on sinning, so that grace may increase? By no means!' (AV 'God forbid'). 'We died to sin, how can we live in it any longer?' (Rom. 6:1-2). We who are truly justified by faith are also horrified at the suggestion that we may continue to live in sin.

In spite of this, it is astonishing how many Christians, after studying what James says about justification by faith, conclude that both faith and deeds are necessary in order to be justified in the sight of God. Such a view totally undermines the gospel. Others, on the presumption that there is a clear contradiction, have foolishly assumed that James does not speak with the same authority as Paul and, therefore, his letter ought not to be in the Scriptures!

Those who reach such unwarranted conclusions have not even understood Paul's doctrine of justification by faith. The first group assume that Paul's dogmatic assertion that 'a man is justified by faith apart from observing the law' (Rom. 3:28) had to be corrected or modified by James, who says 'that a person is justified by what he does and not by faith alone' (James 2:24.). As a result, some use James as a stick to beat Paul, and others use Paul to punish James. It is a clash of ignorance.

I suspect that prejudice against the doctrine of justification by faith alone keeps the conflict alive. Certainly, those who do not like Paul's teaching are fond of quoting James. This only serves to demonstrate the truth of Paul's prediction that 'the time will come when men will not put up with sound doctrine' (2 Tim. 4:3).

Not all, however, are prepared to stand in judgement on Scripture in this way. Those of us who are persuaded that the Scriptures are God's inspired word readily understand that both Paul and James wrote as the Holy Spirit of truth guided them. Therefore, they cannot reveal contradictory doctrines. Where this seems to happen, it is more honouring to God to learn what the apparent contradiction teaches, and how it is to be reconciled, than to hastily accept the one and reject the other.

It is a fixed rule of interpretation that where there appears to be a variation in meaning concerning any doctrine, the classical statement of that doctrine must be paramount. If there is an apparent difference of meaning in other places, we should not assume on first reading that it contradicts the main statement. In this case, it is obvious that the classical statement of the doctrine of justification by faith is contained in

Paul's letters to the Romans. James, on the other hand, is dealing with an abuse of Paul's teaching.

In Rom. 10:1-4, Paul warns of the danger of thinking that our righteousness contributes to our salvation: 'Brothers, my heart's desire and prayer to God for the Israelites is that they may be saved. For I can testify about them that they are zealous for God, but their zeal is not based on knowledge. Since they did not know the righteousness that comes from God and sought to establish their own, they did not submit to God's righteousness. Christ is the end of the law so that there may be righteousness for everyone who believes'.

We must not miss the force of Paul's argument. The Jews were passionate about their religion, but their enthusiasm was no substitute for the knowledge of the truth. In their ignorance, they failed to see that the righteousness of Christ is sufficient and is credited to all who truly believe. They did not understand that being accepted as righteous in God's sight is God's gift. This error had disastrous consequences. It led them to try to establish their own righteousness. Sadly, many have followed their example.

Christ is 'the end of the law' in the sense that the law is abolished as a means of being justified before God. The 'law was put in charge to lead us to Christ' (Gal. 3:24), which means that the commandments exposed our sins and, therefore, our need of Christ. But the law has not been abolished as a rule of life. So there is no comfort here for those antinomians who want to be rid of the law altogether.

What does James mean by 'faith'?

'What good is it, my brothers,' asks James, 'if a man claims to have faith but has no deeds? Can such faith save him?' (James 2:14). The answer to the question is obviously 'No'. In another place, he says: '...faith by itself, if it is not accompanied by action, is dead' (James 2:17). Since true saving faith cannot die and is always accompanied by honourable action, it is obvious that James is using the word 'faith' here in a general sense.

Indeed, when he uses the word on its own, it cannot mean anything more than a mere profession of faith. Even when he refers to Abraham's faith, it seems James is still using the word in this sense. In the event, however, the Patriarch's obedience to God proved it to be otherwise. The same is true of Rahab's profession of faith, although in her case the actual word is not used (James 2:25-26). Rahab did not rise to the height of faithful trust in God as Abraham did, but her action in hiding the spies was a courageous act of faith nevertheless. Her words to the spies show that her act was the fruit of the faith that she already had: '...for the LORD your God is God in heaven above and on the earth below' (Josh. 2:11).

The bottom line is this — faith that does not transform a person's life is not justifying faith. Why? Because faith without deeds is dead, and dead faith does not justify a man before God. It is lifeless and, therefore, useless. We shall see in the next chapter that good deeds are acts of obedience to the word of God. That is to say, they are the fruits of faith. No matter how much 'good' unbelievers may do, it cannot possibly be the fruit of faith.

The good deeds of the justified believer are clearly set out in the Scriptures. They include loving and serving the church of Christ in obedience to God's command (John 13:34), loving and serving my neighbour (Matt. 22:39), forgiving others as God has forgiven me (Matt. 18:21-22), being fair and honest in all my dealings (Rom. 12:17), being a faithful witness for Christ (Matt. 10:32-33), and so on. If these things are not in evidence, then my faith is no better than that of demons. They believe in God and shudder! (James 2:19).

Jesus had to contend with people whose faith was skin deep. As we noted earlier, we are told that when 'many people saw the miraculous signs he was doing' they 'believed in his name. But Jesus would not entrust himself to them, for he knew all men. He did not need man's testimony about man, for he knew what was in a man' (John 2:23-25). Evidently, these people had not believed from the heart. Their faith was merely intellectual.

At one stage in my early childhood, I thought of every good deed I did as another brick in my house in heaven. I used to imagine that thunder was the noise of someone's house in heaven falling down! Childish idea you say, but the fact is that I have known many people — even church people — who think along these lines. In their view, heaven is a reward for their goodness. Even though they had no love for Christ or for his followers, they strongly resented any suggestion that they were not good enough to go to heaven. This is how dead faith behaves.

Paul strongly opposes this self-righteous attitude: 'For if a law had been given that could impart life, then righteousness would certainly have come by the law. But the Scripture declares that the whole world is a prisoner of sin, so that what was promised, being given through faith in Jesus Christ, might be given to those who believe' (Gal. 3:21-22).

We must be clear about this. If God had given us commandments that we could keep, heaven would be the reward of our obedience. But no such law has been given. The law as it stands, has been kept by no one. The standard is unreachable so that, by nature, we are all the prisoners of sin.

We should also note carefully what James says about Abraham: 'Was not our ancestor Abraham considered righteous for what he did when he offered his son Isaac on the altar? You see that his faith and his actions were working together, and his faith was made complete by what he did'. Then he adds: 'the Scripture was fulfilled that says, "Abraham believed God and it was credited to him as righteousness," and he was called God's friend' (James 2:21-23).

In what sense was Abraham's faith made complete? James is not disagreeing with the statement that Abraham's faith 'was credited to him as righteousness'. The apostle is simply saying that these words of Scripture were fulfilled because Abraham proved the genuineness of his faith by his obedience to God. If this had not been the case, the Scripture could not have been fulfilled for the simple reason we mentioned earlier — that dead faith is not justifying faith.

According to Article 12 of the Church of England, 'a lively faith may be as evidently known as a tree is discerned by its fruits'. This statement cannot possibly refer to God as the one who is doing the discerning because he knows the nature of the tree *before* it bears fruit. God also knows the motives of people who do good deeds. It is obvious, therefore, that the Article is talking about the evidence of a living faith as it is presented to the world.

Now, let us suppose I plant an apple tree in my garden. It is a perfectly good tree and I am happy with it. It begins to produce blossom and I watch in amazement as the apples form. This proves to me that the tree is not dead and is doing what a good apple tree is supposed to do. I could say that by bearing fruit the tree was made complete. Everyone who passes by can see that nothing is lacking. It is obviously a genuine, fruit-bearing apple tree

In the same way, Abraham's obedience made his faith complete. That is to say, it proved that his faith was genuine. There was nothing wrong with his faith before, but now we have the evidence that it was genuine. There is no suggestion that he was legally justified before God by his act of obedience. Rather, the act of obedience was proof that he was justified.

If, then, we are to be assured that our faith is genuine, it must pass all the tests that God sends our way. Peter tells his readers that although they greatly rejoice in their salvation, they 'may have had to suffer grief in all kinds of trials. These have come so that your faith — of greater worth than gold ... may be proved genuine and may result in praise, glory and honour when Jesus Christ is revealed' (1 Peter 1:6-7).

To whom is James writing?

Let us suppose you are a traffic policeman and have been detailed to give a lecture on the relationship between speed and safety on the road. On enquiry, you discover that most of your audience will be made up of older drivers who seldom exceed the speed limit and drive slowly on busy motorways. You would need to point out that such behaviour is dangerous and causes difficulty for the following traffic. If, on the other hand, you were informed that your hearers were young road hogs who regularly exceeded the seventy miles an hour limit, your emphasis would have to be very different.

Paul and James are addressing very different 'audiences'. Even in his letter to the Romans, Paul's emphasis is not the same as it is in Galatians. In Romans, he is setting out the classic doctrine of justification by faith. He has no axe to grind because he is not aware of any problem in the Roman church. In his letter to the Galatians, however, he is addressing a serious problem. The Galatians were influenced by false teachers who were insisting that it was not enough merely to trust in Christ; they must observe the law as well. In order to be true Christians they must be circumcised as the law required.

The apostle James has yet another 'audience' in mind. He is not explaining how a person may be justified before God, but warning those who profess to be justified but still live in sin and selfishness. He insists that their claim is false and their faith is dead. They are deceiving no one but themselves.

It would be a big mistake to assume that James is addressing an imaginary problem. Across the world there are millions who suppose that the faith they profess will save them even though they continue to live corrupt lives. Quite rightly, then, James is concerned to establish the principle that all who claim to be justified by faith before God must prove it by the way they live. What genuine believer would not be concerned

to expose the vanity of pretence? After all, it is just as important for James to warn false professors of the danger they are
in as it is for Paul to explain how sinners may be made
acceptable to a holy God.

Conclusion

Christ's righteousness stands between God's judgement and
the believer's unrighteousness. Being shielded from the divine
wrath that would otherwise come upon him, he may stand
boldly before God on the Day of Judgement, knowing that no
one will be able to bring a successful charge against him
(Rom. 8:33). 'For just as through the disobedience of the one
man the many were made sinners, so also through the
obedience of the one man the many will be made righteous'
(Rom. 5:19). Christ's perfect obedience has changed our legal
status before God forever.

Nothing that James says alters this fact. From the believer's
point of view, however, assurance of the fact depends largely
on the evidence of a transformed life. Those readers who
think they can gain favour with God by what they do should
study Paul. Those who think they are true believers, but
whose lives have not changed, should study Paul *and* James.
They should know that the idea that a man may live in sin
and then partake of heaven's joys hereafter is abhorrent to
both.

The words of Calvin in this matter are well known: 'It is
faith alone which justifies, and yet the faith which justifies is
not alone.'

12.

Good deeds

We do not make requests of you because we are righteous,
but because of your great mercy. (Dan. 9:18)

Before conversion

Little Jack Horner sat in a corner, eating a Christmas pie; he
put in his thumb and pulled out a plum, and said, 'What a
good boy am I!' It is often said that many of these old, apparently childish rhymes are based on actual historical people
and events. According to one source, the nursery rhyme dates
from the time when King Henry VIII was getting rid of the
monasteries. Jack Horner, a servant of the Abbot of Glaston-
bury, obtained the deeds of a Manor House by deception.
Along with other documents, they were being sent to the king
hidden in a plum pie and Horner was the courier. At a
convenient point, he lifted the crust and removed the
deeds — the plum!

As it stands, the rhyme does not give us a clue as to why
Horner felt the need to congratulate himself. After all, there is
no virtue in sticking one's thumb into a Christmas pie in order
to steal! But then, people have some rather strange ideas as
to what constitutes goodness. Jack himself, according to the

above story, thought of himself as a good boy when, in fact, he was a thoroughly bad one.

We have said a lot in this book about our 'good' deeds not being good enough for God. This chapter brings the various strands together for the benefit of those readers who are not fully persuaded about the truth of the saying 'by faith alone, through grace alone, in Christ alone'. They will have all the information they need in one place.

I stress this Scripture teaching because I have found that, human nature being what it is, there is a deep-seated reluctance to accept it. The main reason for this resistance is that we are prone to judge God by our standards instead of allowing him to judge us by his. As long as this attitude prevails, there cannot be any genuine repentance and, therefore, no forgiveness.

We need to ponder the word of the Lord to the prophet Isaiah: 'Let the wicked forsake his way and the evil man his thoughts. Let him turn to the LORD, and he will have mercy on him, and to our God, for he will freely pardon... As the heavens are higher than the earth, so are my ways higher than your ways and my thoughts than your thoughts' (Isa. 55:7,9).

Whether we like it or not, the people who are described as wicked and evil in these verses include you and me. That is how God sees us in our natural condition. The deeds of sinful human beings may be considered good in the eyes of other sinful human beings, but God does not see them in this way. The reason is simple: they are not done as he expects them to be done.

The Bible is frank: 'All of us have become like one who is unclean, and all our righteous acts are like filthy rags' (Isa. 64:6). What the prophet is saying here is that those actions we think are righteous are filthy in God's sight. The prophet probably had in mind the soiled cloths used by women during menstruation, which in ancient Israel was considered a defilement. It is a graphic description of God's loathing of the 'good' actions of people who do not obey the gospel. Now, unless and until we accept God's verdict, we shall never make any progress. It is a hard pill to swallow.

The Psalmist does not mince his words either: 'The LORD looks down from heaven on the sons of men to see if there are any who understand, any who seek God. All have turned aside, they have together become corrupt; there is no-one who does good, not even one' (Ps. 14:2-3). Paul quotes these verses in answer to the question: 'Can a person be justified on the basis of his own righteousness?' His conclusion is emphatic: 'No-one will be declared righteous in his sight by observing the law; rather, through the law we become conscious of sin' (Rom. 3:20). What could be clearer?

Romans 8:6-8 confirms this: 'The mind of sinful man is death … the sinful mind is hostile to God. It does not submit to God's law, nor can it do so. Those controlled by the sinful nature cannot please God'. If a forceful denial of the notion that men can earn their own salvation were needed, here we have it. It is impossible for a person under condemnation to merit God's favour no matter what he does or does not do.

For those who have links with the Church of England, Article 13 is emphatic. It may be written in outdated English but the truth it presents is by no means obsolete: 'Works done before the grace of Christ, and the inspiration of His Spirit, are not pleasant to God, forasmuch as they spring not of faith in Jesus Christ... yea, rather, for that they are not done as God hath willed and commanded them to be done, we doubt not but that they have the nature of sin.'

The Article was directed against the teaching of the Roman Catholic Church, which insisted, and still insists, that works done before a man is justified by faith have merit. Although the merit is not considered sufficient to earn salvation outright, the 'good' deeds are seen as a necessary preparation for it.

It becomes obvious, therefore, that our failure to accept God's perfect judgement prevents us from making any progress. It is irksome for us to think that the admirable generosity of our unbelieving friends counts for nothing in God's sight. That people who make tremendous sacrifices to help others should not gain favour with God thereby, is distasteful. And we conclude, on our own authority, that if God will not accept people as righteous because we see them as righteous, he must be a very cruel and inconsiderate God.

There is a cure for this mistaken attitude. Let a person have a revelation of God's infinite holiness and he will not be able to utter another word of criticism. Those of us who have been dazzled by the purity of God's being will never again question the way he deals with sinful people.

I do not speak of some private vision or special revelation of God. To be made aware of the holiness of God is the operation of the Holy Spirit. This does not mean that we become like anaesthetized patients on the operating table. The Spirit reveals his holiness to us through the Holy Scriptures, not least in God's commandments. If we really want to know the holiness of God, we need to pray for the help of his Spirit as we ponder his word. He will not refuse us.

God's holiness, and especially his faultless justice, is also revealed in the death of Christ. Once the Lord Christ had undertaken to pay the price of our sins, his death was inevitable. And the person who understands the immense sacrifice God made to meet his own righteous demands, will never again try to justify himself. He will be surprised at himself for entertaining the idea.

Scripture contains many examples of what happened when God revealed himself to sinful men. No doubt the prophet Isaiah was a jolly good fellow in the eyes of his contemporaries, but, when he saw the Lord, he cried out: 'Woe to me!' and, 'I am ruined! For I am a man of unclean lips...' (Isa. 6:5). Peter, too, when he witnessed Christ's power over nature, said: 'Go away from me, Lord; I am a sinful man!' (Luke 5:8). When the apostle John was confined to the

Isle of Patmos and saw the glory of Christ, he fell at his feet as though dead (Rev. 1:17).

Let it, therefore, be clear in our minds that only those who see what God is really like will see themselves in a true light. Only they will be earnest in their repentance. As long as we think we can put God in our debt, any hope of eternal life will die with us.

After conversion

So far, we have talked about works done before justification. What about those that are done after? They do not earn God's salvation either. How can they possibly contribute to a salvation that is already accomplished? It would be like saying to a child, 'Be a good boy and it will help you to be born'! Those who are born anew of the Spirit of God recognize that their new life is not the cause of their justification but its effect. It cannot be both.

Nevertheless, good works that are the fruit of justification *are* pleasing to God even though they, too, are imperfect. Again, for those readers with an Anglican background, Article 12 spells it out clearly: 'Albeit that Good Works, which are the fruits of Faith, and follow after Justification, cannot put away our sins, and endure the severity of God's Judgement; yet are they pleasing and acceptable to God in Christ, and do spring out necessarily of a true and lively Faith; insomuch that by them a lively Faith may be as evidently known as a tree discerned by the fruit.'

The other day I cleaned the windscreen of my car. When I had finished, it was spotless. At least that is what I thought. The next day, the sun was shining brightly. I reversed the car out of the garage into the sunlight and I could scarcely believe my eyes. Streaks and blemishes were to be seen all over the glass! It is just like this with all our 'good' deeds, even after we have been pardoned. In the light of God's holiness, nothing we do is perfect. But how wonderful it is to know that God is pleased with what we do.

But you may ask how God can be pleased with what is imperfect. He is still the same holy God as he was before we were justified. The truth is, he is not pleased with anything that is imperfect. Nor will he ever be. Our deeds are accepted as perfect in his eyes because all their imperfections are cleansed away by the blood of Christ. God chooses to forget all about them, just as he does with all our sins. That is what being a forgiven sinner means.

Some Christians make the serious mistake of thinking that believing is a meritorious act in itself. That is to say, they think of the exercise of their faith as putting God in their debt. They are saved *because* they have believed. The notion is now so common that new converts take it on board without giving it a thought. But, if we believe that salvation is entirely by grace as the Scripture teaches, how can the exercise of faith be a meritorious work? If, as the apostle says, salvation, including faith, 'is the gift of God' (Eph. 2:8), how can God be in our debt?

Suppose my rich uncle promised to give me a million pounds on my 21st birthday. On the day I receive the cheque, I am foolish enough to write a letter to him with these words: 'Thank you very much uncle for the cheque; it will come in very handy. I really feel I deserve it because I knew you would not go back on your word.' What, do you suppose, my rich uncle would think?

To avoid serious errors of this kind we should understand that it is for the glory of God that justification is entirely of grace. To take any credit for it is to rob him of his glory. Careful reading of Paul's letter to the Ephesians will convince anyone who is not spiritually blind that God's main purpose in our redemption is to bring glory to his Name. He achieves this by turning rotten and incorrigible sinners into saints with no help from them whatsoever.

This was God's purpose from the beginning. He chose us in Christ 'before the creation of the world to be holy and blameless in his sight' (Eph. 1:4) in order that we may be 'to the praise of his glory' (Eph. 1:14). God has raised us up with Christ and seated us with him in the heavenly realms, in order that in the coming ages 'he might show the incomparable riches of his grace, expressed in his kindness to us in Christ Jesus' (Eph. 2:6-7). God's intention is to make his manifold wisdom known to the rulers and authorities in the heavenly realms (Eph. 3:10).

The revelation of Christ as Saviour demonstrated God's perfect justice (Rom. 3:25), displayed his infinite love (1 John 3:16), his grace to the undeserving (Eph. 1:5-6), his many-sided wisdom (1 Cor. 1:24), his absolute power (Rom. 1:16), and his unending faithfulness (Rom. 4:16). Any suggestion that he needs help from his servants is ridiculous.

Loose living

We come back to those people who call themselves Christians but want to cast off all restraint. After all, they say, if having mercy on the sinner brings glory to God, why not go on sinning so that God can go on forgiving? These people work on the principle that justification leaves a person free to do what he likes. Antinomians! Remember? If you want to do it, do it, they say. If we are not saved by our own goodness, what is the point of being good? If all our sins will be forgiven, why bother about righteousness? Sexual morality, honesty and fair play are no longer important.

This is a serious matter. It proves beyond doubt that such people are not Christians at all. To love the Lord Jesus for what he has done to redeem us and to continue in sin is impossible. All who are truly justified are keenly aware of a new and deep-seated desire to glorify God in the way they live. The person who sees nothing wrong in sexual relations outside marriage or in shady business dealings, for example, cannot claim to be a follower of Jesus Christ. God is against people who live like this.

The apostle Paul is careful to block this kind of reasoning. 'Shall we go on sinning, so that grace may increase? By no means!' (Rom. 6:1-2). 'Shall we sin because we are not under law but under grace? By no means!' (Rom. 6:15). No matter how religious a person may be, if he does not live a morally upright life, his religion is false. The believer may fall, but he will get up again. But those who claim to be saved by grace and continue in sin provoke the Lord to anger and are guilty of perverting the Scriptures to their own destruction.

A report by Andrew King in the July 2006 edition of 'Evangelicals Now' on the situation in Brazil contains the following account. It makes sad reading: 'We sometimes wonder aloud, how can there be so little impact at a social level in a country where the evangelical church already includes 20% of the population and is still growing? There is something very seriously wrong with this church growth. There is something seriously wrong with the church.'

'Where does the problem start?' Andrew asks. 'When businessmen routinely falsify the salary figures for their employees in order to reduce tax bills — and Christians do *exactly* the same ... when a pastor can ask for a discount at the recent Colloquium conference, on the basis that he is only coming for one day ... and then having got his badge, attends every day ... when three girls at the same event can say at the registration desk that they have spoken to the organizers and been promised a discount, when no such conversation has taken place.'

It gets worse — 'when a way can be found to pass students in the Bible Institute even when they have failed their exams ... when lack of integrity is so endemic in society that even evangelicals are corrupt without blinking ... when (Isa. 59:14) justice is driven back, and righteousness stands at a distance;

truth has stumbled in the streets, honesty cannot enter ...
when these things rule, it is not surprising to find a great deal
of blood in the same streets.'

In the light of this disturbing report, how thankful true believers ought to be that justice comes from God and that he is
fair and equitable in all his dealings. What a privilege it is to
be created in his image — not physically, but intellectually
and morally. How precious are the God-given virtues of
integrity, purity and honour! Above all, how grateful we are
that God has saved us in order to make us like Jesus. And
what benefits we enjoy by living under his rules right now!
God's law 'is holy, and the commandment is holy, righteous
and good' (Rom. 7:12).

A child who lives in a family where there are rules is far
more secure than the one who belongs to a family where
there are none. Law is necessary for our happiness and well
being. Most human beings strongly disapprove when justice
miscarries. Why then would Christians, of all people, rebel
against living under God's laws and bring the gospel into
disrepute?

Antinomians completely misunderstand the purpose of the
gospel. They ignore the vital link between justification and
sanctification. They must surely know that when Paul spoke
about the 'freedom we have in Christ' (Gal. 2:4), he was not
speaking about freedom *to* sin, but freedom *from* sin —
freedom to do the will of God. We have been set free from
slavery to sin, free from the condemnation of the law, so that
we may be free to serve the living God — something we
could not do before.

Therefore, let no one think he is justified by faith if he has
nothing to show for it. 'Who may ascend the hill of the LORD?
Who may stand in his holy place? He who has clean hands
and a pure heart, who does not lift up his soul to an idol or
swear by what is false' (Ps. 24:3-4).

The call to holy living

About sixty years ago, I had a friend who ran an old car. He always referred to it as 'Dorcas'. If asked why, he would say that it was 'full of good works'. In those days, we all used the Authorized Version of the Bible. In the Acts of the Apostles, we read about a disciple named Tabitha whose Greek name was Dorcas. She is described as a woman who was 'full of good works' (Acts 9:36, Authorized Version). The New International Version translates it, 'always doing good and helping the poor'.

The man's sense of humour highlighted a problem we had and still have with the word 'works'. Today we use the word 'deeds' or 'actions' instead, although 'works' is retained in several places even in the more modern versions of the Bible. Romans 4:2 for example: 'If, in fact, Abraham was justified by works, he had something to boast about — but not before God'.

Readers who have come this far, however, will not be in doubt about the meaning of the word. They should understand by now that every believer is called to what we might call the ministry of good works. They will also know that good works are the fruits of faith and, as such, they are acceptable to God in Christ.

Although justification and sanctification must never be confused, they cannot be separated. When God justifies the sinner, he sanctifies him in two ways. The first is an act of God whereby the forgiven sinner is set apart from the rest of sinful humanity. Because he now belongs to Christ, God regards him as holy. The second is a process of lifelong renewal in the sinner.

This holy calling is stressed all through the Scriptures. We are 'called to be saints' (Rom. 1:7). Saints are not dead people who have been canonized by the Roman Catholic Church, but holy people who are very much alive. We are

'sanctified in Christ Jesus and called to be holy...'
(1 Cor. 1:2). Preparation for the glory to come begins right
now. We 'are being transformed into his likeness with ever-
increasing glory' (2 Cor. 3:18). What a wonderful thing this
is — we progress from one degree of glory into another until
at last we see Jesus and are transformed into his perfect
likeness (1 John 3:2).

It is essential to remember that holiness is primarily a matter of the heart and concerns the private and inner life of the
believer. This is where good deeds originate. His desire is to
use his time and talents, not to set himself on a pedestal, but
to bring honour to his Saviour. Jesus taught us that it is out of
the overflow of the heart that the mouth speaks (Matt. 12:34).
If a man has a foul mouth, he has a foul heart. If, on the other
hand, there is grace in his heart, there will be grace on his
lips. 'Above all else, guard your heart,' says the Book of
Proverbs, 'for it is the wellspring of life' (Prov. 4:23).

Matthew Arnold (1822-1888) is quoted by Anglican theologian Griffith Thomas as saying that conduct is 'three-
quarters of life'. But, as Thomas comments, this entirely begs
the question of the other quarter. 'We might as well say that a
building is three-quarters and the foundation only one quarter
of the entire structure; and yet obviously the former rests
upon the latter.' (W. H. Griffith Thomas, *The Principles of
Theology*, Church Book Room Press Ltd., 1956, pages 213-
214.)

The ever-increasing joy of knowing that God has called us
to spend every moment living for him cannot be described.
Those who experience it would not go back to the fleeting
pleasures of sin if they were offered the whole world.

The features of good deeds

The first and most important feature of good deeds, therefore, is that they glorify God. As Jesus said: 'Let your light shine before men, that they may see your good deeds and praise your Father in heaven' (Matt. 5:16). There is no telling what effect a compassionate act may have on an unbeliever. Not that we have an ulterior motive in helping others. Our reason for doing it is the same as that of Jesus: 'When he saw the crowds, he had compassion on them, because they were harassed and helpless, like sheep without a shepherd' (Matt. 9:36).

Secondly, love for Christ must be the essential motive. To expect God to accept deeds that spring from any other motive is a forlorn hope. Love for Christ inevitably means love for Christians and, therefore, we shall be careful to give them priority. Paul puts it like this: 'Therefore, as we have opportunity, let us do good to all people, especially to those who belong to the family of believers' (Gal. 6:10).

Helping the family of believers, or anyone else for that matter, does not consist only in giving food to the physically hungry, but also in providing spiritual food for the spiritually hungry. Obviously, nothing is to be gained by depriving anyone of their physical needs (James 2:15-16) if we have the ability to meet them. But the more serious deprivation is to leave them in ignorance of the gospel.

The Westminster Confession of 1647 provides us with an excellent definition of good works. Section 1 tells us that 'good works are only such as God has commanded in his Holy Word'. That is to say, the deed must be something that God wants us to do. The reason for this is that, since God is the source of all goodness, a deed cannot be good unless it is done in the way God approves. The Confession goes on to explain that good works, 'done in obedience to God's commandments, are the fruits and evidences of a true and lively faith'.

The fundamental difference, therefore, between deeds done before and after justification is the fact that the former originate in man but the latter in God. This is the teaching of the apostle: 'For we are God's workmanship, created in Christ Jesus to do good works, which God prepared in advance for us to do' (Eph. 2:10). God has made us what we are so that we shall fulfil his purpose for our lives on earth. The fact that God planned our good deeds in advance is another reason why they cannot contribute to our salvation: 'For those God foreknew he also predestined to be conformed to the likeness of his Son...' (Rom. 8:29).

Although the duty of doing good is obligatory for everyone, for the Christian it is more than just duty. It is an expression of gratitude. If we love Jesus for what he has done, we will willingly do what he says (John 14:15). 'I want you to stress these things,' says Paul, 'so that those who have trusted in God may be careful to devote themselves to doing what is good' (Titus 3:8).

What are 'these things' that Titus must stress, and why should he stress them? Paul has just been speaking about the kindness and love of God who saved us, 'not because of righteous things we had done, but because of his mercy' (Titus 3:4-5). Paul also reminds Titus of the generous outpouring of the Holy Spirit upon us 'so that, having been justified by his grace, we might become heirs having the hope of eternal life' (Titus 3:7). Titus must stress these things so that those who believe 'may be careful to devote themselves to doing what is good'. They must see their lives as an expression of gratitude.

The true Christian's ongoing life of righteousness will stand throughout his life as evidence that he 'who began a good work in you will carry it on to completion until the day of Christ Jesus' (Phil. 1:6). The believer himself is the primary

witness of the miracle which is constantly taking place under
his own nose!

'May the God of peace, who through the blood of the
eternal covenant brought back from the dead our Lord Jesus,
that great Shepherd of the sheep, equip you with everything
good for doing his will, and may he work in us what is pleasing to him, through Jesus Christ, to whom be glory for ever
and ever. Amen' (Heb. 13:20-21).

13.

Perfect freedom

It is for freedom that Christ has set us free. (Gal. 5:1)

Freedom and authority

A visit to the number of 'freedom' organizations advertising on the Internet is enough to persuade anyone that the meaning of the word is what we make it. 'Freedom,' says the establishment known as Freedom House, 'is possible only in democratic political systems in which governments are accountable to their own people; the rule of law prevails; and freedoms of expression, association, belief and respect for the rights of minorities and women are guaranteed.'

At the other extreme, 'Freedom' is the name given to an anarchist newspaper. The organization, based in London, claims that it is 'the world's oldest Anarchist publisher'. So we have a conflict about the meaning at once, Freedom House insisting that there is no freedom except under the law, and the anarchists maintaining the exact opposite.

To discover the meaning of the word 'freedom' in any given context, we need to pose the question: 'Freedom from what to do what?' That is to say, we need to know what precisely the tyranny is from which we need to be freed, and what the result will be if and when we are set free from it. If we make a mistake here and start demanding freedom from the restrictions of a just and necessary law, the tyranny of the imagined freedom will be far worse than the limits imposed on our freedom by that law.

At the present time, I think the majority in Britain would agree that freedom of religion, freedom from want, freedom from fear, freedom of speech and so forth demands the protection of the law. If we already enjoy these freedoms, it is our duty to do everything we can to preserve them. There are, however, increasing numbers of people who want to break free from the restraints of the law. Some would like to get rid of our democratic system altogether. They would willingly reverse the emancipation of women and put an end to free speech. That the law prevents these people having their way is something for which we should be thankful.

It is all a question of authority. Seemingly blind to the benefits of living under authority, whether it is that of parents, school teachers or the police, many now see authority itself as the enemy of freedom. 'Who gives this person or this group of people the right to tell me what I can or cannot do?'

Wisdom dictates, however, that freedom and authority belong together. Imagine the chaos that would result if all authority were abolished. If we have suffered at the hands of tyrannical parents or crooked police officers, the answer is not to get rid of all parents and all police officers but to try to eliminate the injustices. If we allow those who use their authority badly to fuel the fires of contempt for the law, we shall all be the losers.

What seems to have been forgotten by the agitators is that freedom to please myself is bondage of the worst kind. I become a slave to my own passions and lusts. I reach the point where I crave for freedom, not now from the law, but from my sinful self. Freedom from myself, however, is something I am powerless to achieve. If I emigrate to the other side of the world to 'get away from it all', as the saying goes, I shall find that I have taken my problems with me. Whatever we do, we remain slaves to sin, and Christ is the only one who can break the chains and set us free.

When we speak of Christian freedom, therefore, God's law, and man-made laws that conform to it, present no problem for the believer.

The slavery of sin

I recall seeing for the first time the fairly well-known drawing illustrating the way in which slaves were packed into British slave ships. These ships plied along the African coast taking black men and women by force from their homes to forced labour in the British colonies. Whenever I think of the picture I feel a sense of shame that the people of my own race would sink to this level for the sake of money. The slaves were brutally treated. They were whipped, branded and kept in chains. Many died on the voyage and their bodies were just thrown overboard into the Atlantic Ocean. It is estimated that between 1579 and 1807 more than 15,000,000 slaves were taken from Africa to the Americas.

What a day of rejoicing it must have been when, on the first day of August 1834 the Emancipation Act was passed and slavery abolished throughout the British Empire. In the West Indies, three quarters of a million people were suddenly set free. Yet, the cruelty and inhumanity of the trade still tarnishes the history of Britain.

But slavery to sin is a form of slavery far worse than this. It is particularly dangerous because sin's slaves are duped into thinking that they are free. I am reminded of a man who said: 'I can stop smoking any time I want'. There was only one snag — he never wanted! He was in the iron grip of his addiction. So it is with slaves to sin. Because, in the initial stages, sin is attractive and pleasurable to our sinful nature, we are captivated by it. Naturally, we have no desire to break free.

It is the nature of everyone born into this world to commit sin. According to James, each person 'is tempted when, by his own evil desire, he is dragged away and enticed. Then, after desire has conceived, it gives birth to sin; and sin, when it is full-grown, gives birth to death' (James 1:14-15). Every living creature behaves as its nature dictates and human beings are no exception. The apple tree is not an apple tree just because it grows apples. On the contrary, it grows apples because it is an apple tree. Apples are in its nature. In the same way, we are not sinners because we sin. Rather, we sin because we are sinners. To sin is in our nature and we can do no other.

We are not thinking here only about sin as an occasional act of disobedience but as a power that holds everyone in the world in bondage. Even God's redeemed people are not free from it as long as they remain in this body. The difference in their case is that they are no longer under its curse. This is the diagnosis of God's word. To refuse to accept it is to contradict God himself.

Jesus spoke of the slavery to sin when he said: 'I tell you the truth, everyone who sins is a slave to sin' (John 8:34). What did he mean? He was not talking about an isolated sin in an otherwise holy life but about the habit of sinning from which we all suffer by nature. Nor was he talking about anti-social thugs who take particular pleasure in breaking the law. Jesus is saying that all who are unable to break free from the habit of sinning — and that includes everyone — are slaves to sin. By nature, sin is our master. We cannot break free from its chains.

We said just now that many think of liberty as release from the authority of parents and the police and even the authority of the State. That is bad enough, but even worse is the notion that liberty consists in freedom from God's law. Who says I must not commit adultery? If my neighbour's wife enjoys it as much as I do, not even God has the right to tell me I should not do it! And if a lie or two improves my career prospects, why should I be held back by an ancient commandment that forbids false witness?

In the nature of the case, if we consider ourselves free to flout divine law, the chains of sin become stronger. Its attraction will lead us further and further up a blind alley where its pleasures will eventually fade and die. All our hopes of freedom will be dashed and we shall be brought down to the dust of death and eternal destruction.

Those who incline to the view that Scripture's lurid descriptions of sin and its effect apply only to muggers, rapists, robbers, murderers and the like, need to take a fresh look at its teaching. The people whom Jesus branded as the children of the devil were very respectable people. To the highly regarded Pharisees he said: 'You belong to your father, the devil, and you want to carry out your father's desire' (John 8:44). Do not be deceived. Many respectable people are walking around with the iron ball of unforgiven sin chained to their ankles.

If we are to make progress in knowing the freedom truth brings, we simply must face the fact of sin. We are all held captive, for 'the Scripture declares that the whole world is a prisoner of sin...' (Gal. 3:22). The words 'the whole world' include princes and paupers, presidents and priests. There are no exceptions.

The words 'prisoner of sin' in the above verse are a form of shorthand. As the Scriptures explain, it is not sin in itself but God's law that has the power to hold us prisoner. Sin derives its power from God's commandments. Let me illustrate the point. If I were found guilty of assault, it would not be my crime that keeps me in prison, but the power of the law. If there were no law against assault, I would not be in jail because in the eyes of the law I would not be guilty of anything. But it is not the fault of the law that I am in custody. The fault is entirely mine. I am the evil party, not the law.

The same applies to God's law. Paul is explicit: 'What shall we say, then? Is the law sin? Certainly not! Indeed I would not have known what sin was except through the law' (Rom. 7:7). 'So then, the law is holy, and the commandment is holy, righteous and good' (Rom. 7:12).

It is from this condemnation of God's law that Christ came to set us free, so that we may become slaves to God. Slaves to God! Does this sound dreadful to you? If so, it proves you have no experience of it. To be God's slave is the most glorious freedom known to man — so glorious that words cannot describe it. But we are going to try anyway.

Freedom in Christ

Being justified by faith brings freedom from condemnation that cannot be obtained in any other way. It is far more precious than any other kind of freedom. The freedoms we enjoy in this world are for a time only. Freedom in Christ is for eternity. It is the gift of God himself and, once received, no one can take it away. It begins at the moment God sets us free from the penalty of sin and will reach its most splendid and permanent state when we see Jesus in his glory.

Being free from condemnation means that we are free from guilt and the fear of death. It means freedom from the control of sin, 'For sin shall not be your master' (Rom. 6:14). Ultimately, it means freedom from decay, pain and spiritual death, and freedom from the very presence of sin. The privilege and joy of being Christ's captives — or perhaps better — being captivated by Christ — is known only by those who experience it. The 1662 Book of Common Prayer rightly describes God's service as 'perfect freedom'.

A colleague of mine, the vicar of a neighbouring parish, had been providing breakfast for a vagrant every Wednesday morning. He arrived about nine o'clock. One morning he arrived late, just as the vicar and his wife were leaving to attend a funeral. 'Sorry,' the vicar said, 'you'll have to wait until we come back.' 'But I'm hungry,' the man replied angrily. When my friend returned, the tramp had put the dustbin lid through the kitchen window. The police were called but there was nothing they could do. The tramp had no money to pay for the damage, and they would not put him in jail because that was just what he wanted. The poor man did not want his freedom because he did not know what to do with it.

Those who are justified by faith do not have this problem. Being free to serve the Lord — something we could not do when we were the objects of his wrath — is a full-time job. There is so much to do, and time is precious. Even at my age, I still have the desire to use every waking moment to bring honour to the Lord Jesus Christ.

'When you were slaves to sin,' wrote Paul to the Romans, 'you were free from the control of righteousness.' Freedom from the control of righteousness is both deadly and degrading. Paul goes on to explain: 'What benefit did you reap at that time', he asks, 'from the things you are now ashamed of? Those things result in death! But now that you have been set free from sin and have become slaves to God, the benefit you reap leads to holiness, and the result is eternal life' (Rom. 6:20-22).

This, then, is the paradox — those who think they are free are slaves to sin, and those who know they are slaves to Christ are free men. Freedom to do as I please is slavery of the worst kind and leads to eternal death; freedom to please God means holy living and leads to eternal life. These two alternatives are set before us, and every one of us will have to choose one or the other.

Make me a captive Lord, and then I shall be free;
Force me to render up my sword, and I shall conqueror be.

(George Matheson 1842-1906)

14.

God's covenant

He remembers his covenant for ever... the covenant he made with Abraham, the oath he swore to Isaac. He confirmed it to Jacob as a decree, to Israel as an everlasting covenant. (Ps. 105:8-10)

Since this subject has no direct link with Justification by Faith, the reader may wonder why I have included it. The reason is simple. One of my main concerns is that believers should feel secure in their faith, and the assurance that we are justified is impossible unless we are persuaded that God does not change his mind. A brief study of the Covenants of the Bible will greatly strengthen our confidence in this matter.

True, there are places in Scripture where God is said to regret doing something because of the evil of men. For example, we read in Genesis 6:6 that, because of man's wickedness, 'the LORD was grieved that he had made man on the earth, and his heart was filled with pain'.

That this is just a human way of expressing God's reaction to the wickedness of men is proven by 1 Samuel 15:28-29. Samuel said to King Saul: 'The LORD has torn the kingdom of Israel from you today and has given it to one of your neighbours — to one better than you. He who is the Glory of

Israel does not lie or change his mind; for he is not a man, that he should change his mind'.

Yet, in the same chapter we are told that 'the LORD was grieved that he had made Saul king over Israel' (1 Sam. 15:35). Are we, then, to assume that God, who does not repent, repented of making Saul king? It may appear like this to us — hence the human form of explanation — but it was Saul who chose to do evil. The only change of mind is in men. But failure on our part does not force a change of plan on God's part. God does not change (Mal. 3:6). No one can fully understand this. But then, who can understand God's ways?

Dispensationalism

Every student of the Bible should realize that there are a variety of ways of reading it. For example, the people known as dispensationalists believe that Bible history is divided into different periods, called dispensations. Supporters of the theory claim that it is the best way to understand the different ways God has worked throughout history.

Although dispensationalists differ as to how many dispensations there are, the following will provide the reader with a general outline. First, we have the dispensation of innocence, before Adam fell into sin. Second, the dispensation of conscience, from Adam to Noah. Third, the dispensation of government from Noah to Abraham. Fourth, the dispensation of patriarchal rule, from Abraham to Moses. Fifth, the dispensation of law, from Moses to Christ. Sixth is the dispensation of grace and the Millennium, number seven.

Dispensationalism began with John Nelson Darby (1800-1882), one of the founders of the Plymouth Brethren (a break-away from the Brethren movement founded by A. A. Groves). Darby saw Bible history as being divided into different periods of time with a different way of salvation in each. Man was put to the test in each period and, as each ended in failure, God brought in a new arrangement and the process started all over again.

To illustrate the point, God promised to give the Jews a kingdom on this earth but, when they rejected Christ, the promise could not be fulfilled and had to be set aside. Then, the dispensation of grace came in and the church was founded instead. The establishment of the church could not, therefore, be foreseen in the Old Testament. Indeed, nothing could be foreseen because everything rested on man's response.

C. I. Scofield (1843-1921), an American pastor, produced *The Scofield Reference Bible*. It is the Authorized Version with Scofield's notes at the bottom of the page. The publication of this Bible gave dispensationalism a big boost, especially in America, and it is still very much alive.

The idea that there have been different ways of salvation is, in itself, a sufficient reason for rejecting this teaching. True Christianity has always taught that there is only one way of being saved and it has never changed. Even though the dispensationalists claim that there is progression from one period to the next, this, evidently, is not the case. True progression is a movement towards a fuller revelation, not a different one. On the dispensationalist theory, once the train hits the buffers, the journey has to begin all over again.

When the latest and most advanced car rolls off the production line, it is not a totally new concept. It is a further development in the history of the motorcar. The principles governing the production of all previous models have not been abolished, but improved. It is not necessary to re-invent the motorcar in order to develop it.

Dispensationalists, however, reject the view that the various covenants we read about in the Bible belong together and develop the same truths. According to Darby, the covenants God established with men were not related to each other in any meaningful sense. They cannot, therefore, be seen as having a single purpose — the unfolding of God's eternal purpose in redemption.

The influence of the *Scofield Bible* is responsible in a big way for the prevailing notion among Christians that God has abandoned the Old Testament. The prophet Jeremiah will set us straight on this by showing that the New Covenant is a further development in the revelation of God's purpose: '"The time is coming," declares the LORD, "when I will make a new covenant with the house of Israel and with the house of Judah... This is the covenant that I will make ... I will put my law in their minds and write it on their hearts. I will be their God and they will be my people"' (Jer. 31:31,33).

Not only is the so-called dispensation of the Law developed here, but the very same promise given to Abraham is again repeated. That little rhyme I learned so many years ago comes to mind: 'The New is in the Old concealed; the Old is in the New revealed'.

The covenants

Another, and much better, way of reading the Scriptures is to take the everlasting covenant as our starting point. I use the singular because the various covenants all belong together, especially from Abraham onwards. The covenant with Abraham, often referred to as the Covenant of Grace, and the covenant with Moses (The Mosaic Covenant), are not different ways of being saved. Rather, they are successive developments of gospel truth.

That the covenant with Abraham is everlasting and cannot be abolished or superseded is clear from Hebrews 6:14-17. Referring to the covenant, the writer says: 'Because God wanted to make the unchanging nature of his purpose clear to the heirs of what was promised, he confirmed it with an oath'.

And why did God do this? 'So that, by two unchangeable things' (the promise and the oath) 'in which it is impossible for God to lie, we who have fled to take hold of the hope offered to us may be greatly encouraged' (Heb. 6:18).

And why were the Israelites delivered from the bondage of Egypt under the leadership of Moses? God appeared to Moses and said: 'I have heard the groaning of the Israelites, whom the Egyptians are enslaving, and I have remembered my covenant' (Exod. 6:5). God is speaking of the covenant made with Abraham, Isaac and Jacob.

Enough has been said to encourage the reader to follow the way in which the will of God is progressively revealed in the covenants. If their purpose is to reveal God's unchanging truth, they must belong together and be everlasting in nature. Each one is a fuller and, therefore, a better revelation than its predecessor, and no covenant makes the previous one void.

Obviously, God's covenants are made with people in time — Adam, Noah, Abraham, Moses, David and so on. The most important covenant of all, however, was established in eternity — or, as the Scripture has it, before the creation of the world. This covenant, usually known as the Covenant of Redemption, overarches all the other covenants. Indeed, all the covenants made between God and men are the outworking of the Covenant of Redemption.

Although this covenant is not mentioned directly in the Scriptures, it is clearly taught. It is a covenant made between the Persons of the Trinity. In brief, we may say that God the Father was the Planner, God the Son undertook to be the Redeemer, and the Holy Spirit became the Executor. The elect — those who were predestined for glory — were given to Jesus as a precious gift.

Many verses in the Gospel of John record what Jesus had to say about this. Here are just a few: 'I have food to eat that you know nothing about' (John 4:32). '"My food," said Jesus, "is to do the will of him who sent me and to finish his work"' (John 4:34. See also 6:38; 7:16-18; 14:30-31; 8:16; 11:42;

17:3). Those who accept Jesus also accept the Father who sent him: 'I tell you the truth, whoever accepts anyone I send accepts me; and whoever accepts me accepts the one who sent me' (John 13:20). And those who accept him were chosen before the creation of the world (Eph. 1:4). It is to these people that Jesus reveals himself: 'I have revealed you to those whom you gave me out of the world. They were yours; you gave them to me...' (John 17:6. See also verse 24).

These texts, and many more, provide overwhelming evidence for the Covenant of Redemption. The sole purpose of the covenant is to glorify both Father and Son by redeeming his elect church and setting the Lord Jesus on the throne of a redeemed universe. The apostle Paul makes it clear that God 'made known to us the mystery of his will according to his good pleasure, which he purposed in Christ, to be put into effect when the times will have reached their fulfilment — to bring all things in heaven and on earth together under one head, even Christ' (Eph. 1:9-10).

Thankfully, unlike human covenants, God's covenants are imposed. He did not ask for our agreement before entering into a covenant relationship with us. This may seem strange when we realize that a covenant is simply an agreement. Marriage, for example, can only take place with the consent of both parties. Nevertheless, those who enter into covenant with God do so willingly because he graciously makes them willing. He imposes conditions and promises blessings, but he never violates our will. We who are called accept the conditions gladly.

One of my hobbies is landscape painting. As a general rule, if I do a quick painting and do not bother too much about the details, the majority of those who comment on it do not like it. They seem to think that a picture that omits the details is not true to life. In fact, I have noticed that when some people view my paintings, the first thing they do is to put their noses a few inches from the paper. They do not stand back to get an overall view. Such people go away with the details in mind, but do not carry away an impression of the entire picture.

A knowledge of the covenant will save us from doing this with the Bible. It will provide us with that small scale map usually found at the beginning of the road atlas. It will show the entire journey we intend to take, from the time our names were written in the book of life (Phil. 4:3) to the place to which we are travelling. Once we have it firmly in mind, all the larger scale pages that show just a part of the journey will make sense because we know how they fit into the big picture. Like those large scale pages, the covenants progress from one era to the next until the whole picture is revealed.

We see, then, that all the covenants point in the same direction. The Covenant of Grace, first established with Abraham and then with Isaac and Jacob; the Covenant with Moses, then David and, of course, the New Covenant, all belong together. Throughout the Bible, we are constantly reminded that God's covenant is everlasting. Abraham is informed of the fact in Genesis 17:13. Moses is reminded of it in Leviticus 24:8. David speaks of it at the end of his life (2 Sam. 23:5).

The Psalmist, too, stresses the unity and permanence of the covenant: 'He is the LORD our God; his judgements are in all the earth. He remembers his covenant for ever, the word he commanded for a thousand generations, the covenant he made with Abraham, the oath he swore to Isaac. He confirmed it to Jacob as a decree, to Israel as an everlasting covenant' (Ps. 105:7-10).

So does Zechariah. When giving thanks for the birth of John the Baptist he makes it clear that the Lord has remembered 'his holy covenant, the oath he swore to our father Abraham...' (Luke 1:72-73).

We see, then, that the Covenant of Grace was not made with Abraham alone, but with all his faithful successors — those who 'walk in the footsteps of the faith that our father

Abraham had before he was circumcised' (Rom. 4:12). The promise that God would be our God, originally made to Abraham, turns out to be a promise for the whole church of Christ (Gen. 17:6-8) because the same promise is made in the New Covenant (Jer. 31:33; 2 Cor. 6:16), reaching its fulfilment in the glory of heaven (Rev. 21:3).

The mediator of the covenant

The writer to the Hebrews refers to the blood of Christ as 'the blood of the eternal covenant' (Heb. 13:20). Jesus is the mediator of the covenant (Heb. 7:22). The gospel promises, offering Christ and his benefits to the sinner are, therefore, invitations to enter and enjoy a covenant relationship with God. When we trust the promises of the gospel, we are not only embracing covenant promises, but entering into the privileged status that God planned for us before time began.

It is evident that the true church of Christ — the fellowship of believers that the gospel creates — is the community of the covenant. It consists of those who are redeemed by faith in Christ. The Bible, of course, is the book of the covenant and heaven is its full and perfect realization (Rev. 21:1-4).

Justification by faith is the only means of salvation throughout. Abraham believed the promises of God and his faith was credited to him as righteousness (Gen. 15:6). King David of Israel was justified by faith. He spoke from experience when he said, 'Blessed is the man whose sin the LORD does not count against him...' (Ps. 32:2).

Therefore, what Christ achieved on the cross is effective for all God's children, whether they lived in 2000BC or 2000AD. The way of salvation for Abraham and for me is exactly the same. We are both justified by faith in Christ. We are both members of the covenant of grace. I know much more about it than Abraham did, but the method remains the same.

The covenants with Adam and Noah

Although the covenant God made with Abraham is seen as the beginning of the everlasting Covenant of Grace, we must not forget the covenant of works made with Adam. We call it the covenant of works because it was based on the principle: 'Do this and you will live' (Gal. 3:12). By contrast, the covenant of grace is based on the principle: 'Repent and believe the good news' (Mark 1:15). The account of the fall of Adam reveals the nature of the human problem. Adam and all his descendants were cut off. Their relationship with God was ruined.

Nor should we overlook the covenant with Noah. This, too, was different. God's promise, that he would never again destroy the world with a flood was not made to a select few, but to the entire future human race.

Both these covenants — the covenants with Adam and Noah — point forward to the covenant of grace. The rudiments of the gospel are contained in the curse put upon the serpent: 'And I will put enmity between you and the woman, and between your offspring and hers; he will crush your head, and you will strike his heel' (Gen. 3:15). And Noah 'became heir of the righteousness that comes by faith' (Heb. 11:7). That is to say, he too was justified by faith, before Abraham.

The covenant with Moses

I deal with this separately because, of all the covenants, it is the most misunderstood. The influence of dispensationalism has caused many believers to think of the Old Testament as being all about the law and the New, all about grace. For them, the record from Genesis to Malachi is an account of God's failed attempt to justify men by their obedience. This is a grave error.

The error is compounded because the Letter to the Hebrews refers frequently to the old covenant, meaning the Mosaic Covenant. The writer even calls it the 'first covenant'. But it is clear that he is referring to the covenant made with Moses and not to the entire Old Testament.

Obviously, although the purpose of the Mosaic covenant was the same, its administration was different, the focus being on the sacrifices, prophecies and circumcision. The sacrifices were accepted by God as a sufficient offering for sin, but only for the time being. Nevertheless, the covenant of grace was still in force. Indeed, right in the middle of the giving of the law to Moses, God promises that if the people repent and confess their sins, 'I will remember my covenant with Jacob and my covenant with Isaac and my covenant with Abraham…' (Lev. 26:42).

In addition, all the sacrifices pointed forward to the coming of the Messiah, the only perfect sacrifice. 'But when this priest had offered for all time one sacrifice for sins, he sat down at the right hand of God' (Heb. 10:12). There was then no further need for animal sacrifice or mediating priests. But what a loss it would have been if we did not have all the types and shadows of the Mosaic law. To be deprived of the rich teaching of the Letter to the Hebrews would have been a great loss.

Conclusion

The believer who reads the Bible for the first time with the unity of the covenants in mind will be surprised how the Old Testament comes alive. This will be particularly so if he has been brought up on the *Scofield Bible*. Because of its wide-spread influence, there are still many believers who try to read the Bible in a dispensational framework. They pay a high price. They cannot see that belonging to Christ means being members of an everlasting covenant. It means having Abraham as our father.

Not only this, but the sheer delight of knowing that God is calling a people to whom he committed himself before the world was made, completely escapes them. Even their understanding of the character of God is adversely affected.

But let them understand that their God is the one who established an everlasting covenant with them, from which all other covenants developed and the scales will fall from their eyes. Everything will come into sharper focus. They will see God in a new and better light and will begin to rejoice as they have never done before, in his everlasting love.

In summary, the covenant approach to Scripture is essential for a proper understanding of the gospel. The Bible is a consistent and progressive revelation of unchanging truth. Jesus Christ has always been the only Saviour and the Covenant of Grace has been ratified by his blood. Justification by faith is, and always has been, the only method by which we may be saved. The Law given to Moses exposes sin and our need of Christ. The sacrifices of the Mosaic covenant were temporary and pointed to the New Covenant. All who are saved, are God's covenanted people. He is our God and we are his people forever — just as he promised.

'Praise be to the Lord, the God of Israel, because he has come and has redeemed his people.
He has raised up a horn of salvation for us in the house of his servant David ... to show mercy to our fathers and to remember his holy covenant, the oath he swore to our father Abraham...'

(Luke 1:68-73)

15.

Test yourself

Examine yourselves to see whether you are in the faith; test yourselves. Do you not realize that Christ Jesus is in you — unless, of course, you fail the test? (2 Cor. 13:5)

What should the test cover?

When I take my car in for its MOT (the Ministry of Transport compulsory annual test), the inspectors are not interested in the cleanliness of the interior upholstery, or the condition of the car radio. Their only concern is to make sure that the car is safe on the road. The brakes, tyres, steering, wheel-bearings, the exhaust system and the state of the bodywork will, therefore, be the focus of their attention.

Similarly, when I submit myself to a test of my spiritual condition, it does not cover things like my hair loss and other signs of ageing. It includes every area of my life over which I have some control and which may, or may not, be honouring to God. How do I use my time and my talents? How do I use my body? What is my attitude to my wife and family and my friends? Am I willing to help and forgive others when they sin against me? How do I give or spend my money?

If there is some cherished sin from which I get pleasure, hidden from public view, it must not be ignored. I must let the light shine into those dark corners where some shameful indulgence may be hiding. As with the MOT, some faults may not be immediately obvious. Others will be clear for all to see.

As we shall see in a moment, the test should also cover my private and my inner life. What do I believe? Do I study God's word and pray regularly? Am I making progress in checking those evil thoughts and fantasies that come into my mind without being invited? Am I taking care to keep my heart pure?

Some may ask why we have to submit to a test? If we have the assurance that we are justified in God's sight and believe his promise to watch over us, what is the point of it? In any case, we do not have the serious problems the church in Corinth had. But this is a serious misunderstanding. The test works both ways. That is to say, it confirms those who are truly in the faith but who may not be sure, and exposes those who think they are but, in reality, are not.

The problem we face is that not many people find self-examination easy. To their great cost, they are not in the habit of searching the Scriptures and, therefore, are not skilled in handling the word of truth correctly (2 Tim. 2:15). The noble example of the Bereans, who made it a rule to study the Scriptures (Acts 17:11), is not followed by many. Even on the part of genuine believers, this slackness so easily becomes a permanent habit. If this is the case, now is the time to start putting it right.

At the outset of the exercise, we must remember three important rules. First, if we are not sure about our status before God at the end of it, it does not *necessarily* mean that our faith is false. Some true believers are inclined to take a dim view of themselves by focussing too much on the negatives. The question posed by Paul: 'Do you not realize that Christ Jesus is in you?' (2 Cor. 13:5) clearly implies that it is possible to have Christ in the heart and not be sure about it. This situation, however, need not continue.

The believer's self-examination will also relate to the fellowship of the church to which he belongs. It is not always realized that, no matter how active a church may appear, her spiritual health depends entirely on the spiritual health of her members. The examination must, of course, be personal for each member. How do I relate to my fellow-believers? Am I eager to promote the church's well being? Am I at home in the fellowship or do I feel like a fish out of water?

Paul says to the church in Rome: '…if anyone does not have the Spirit of Christ, he does not belong to Christ' (Rom. 8:9). My attitude to the worship and fellowship of the church — providing the church is not dead — will provide convincing evidence one way or the other. As a rule, if I have the Spirit of Christ, I shall delight in the company of all who have the same Spirit.

Someone will ask, 'How can I tell the difference between those who belong and those who do not? Is it possible to know the difference between a nominal Christian and a true believer who is troubled with serious doubts?' Admittedly, we are in a difficult area here, but yes, it is possible to know the difference. Speaking from experience, those who are merely nominal Christians do not usually have any concern about their spiritual condition. Since they have not been awakened to their plight, the above questions will not arise. For these people, 'Repent and believe the good news' (Mark 1:15) is the appropriate order of the day.

On the other hand, those who are deeply troubled by their doubts give clear evidence of a desire to be rid of them. This, in itself, is evidence of the work of the Holy Spirit. No one in the wide world is ever troubled about his spiritual status, unless and until the Spirit has enlightened him. The appropriate advice in this case would be to chase the doubts away and follow Paul's example: 'I press on towards the goal to win the prize for which God has called me heavenwards in Christ Jesus' (Phil. 3:14). This may mean some drastic changes in my lifestyle to make sure that the means of grace — worship, prayer, fellowship and sound Bible teaching — are not neglected. Without this change, the doubts may well persist.

The second rule is this: do not expect perfection. Perfection in the believer must wait for the day when he is changed into the likeness of Christ. A few weeks ago, I took my car in for its MOT. The inspector found that my tyres were well worn but still within the legal limit. The rear expansion chamber on the exhaust system had a small hole in it but, since it was not blowing fumes out, that, too, was acceptable. In a similar way, a biblical test of our faith will show up weaknesses but they do not necessarily spell failure.

Nevertheless, these weaknesses must be kept in mind. Just as I, the owner and driver of the car, should remember where the weaknesses are, so, as a believer, I must be watchful of my vulnerable areas. We all have them but not all in the same place.

At this point the car illustration breaks down because, whatever I do with it, I will not be able to stop the rot. Eventually it will end up in the breaker's yard. But the believer is not heading for the scrap heap. True, my body is going the same way as the car, but the new self is 'being renewed in knowledge in the image of its Creator' (Col. 3:10).

I have known Christians who believed in the possibility of sinless perfection in this life. But it was obvious to everyone who knew them that they were deceiving themselves. I recall one woman in particular who always insisted that her quick temper was righteous indignation. That this was a failed attempt to turn a sin into a virtue was obvious to everyone except herself.

This is the third rule: it is the sum total of the evidence that will reveal to me the true state of my heart. Since we are plagued with a sinful nature, it is so easy to think that the areas where I am making good progress will compensate for those where I am not. It is useless, for example, to think that a more generous spirit will cover over my inability to break free from the love of money.

Internal evidence

From time to time, when missing persons are found alive and well, we hear the relatives claiming that they knew all the time that their loved one would eventually be found. What they mean by this is not easy to say. Are they claiming supernatural knowledge of some kind, or is it just a device to bolster their confidence in a desperate situation? All the evidence suggests that it is purely subjective and reflects a dogged determination not to believe the worst, but nothing more.

The assurance believers have that they are the children of God is different. It comes from above and not from within. John refers to it as 'the testimony of God, which he has given about his Son' (1 John 5:9), and goes on to say that 'Anyone who believes in the Son of God has this testimony in his heart' (John 5:10). In the power of the Holy Spirit, what the Scriptures say about the inner life of the believer becomes real.

Paul, too, speaks of this experience. 'The Spirit himself testifies with our spirit that we are God's children' (Rom. 8:16). The inner assurance that God has poured his love into our hearts (Rom. 5:5) is confirmed by the Holy Spirit himself. Words become hopelessly inadequate at this point, but those who experience the inner witness of the Spirit cannot be in any doubt.

Now, if we have the assurance of the Spirit that we are the children of God, why is it necessary to pursue the examination further? Why do we need the further evidence of a changed life to confirm it? But the evaluation of our lives in the light of God's word is not really an alternative or an additional method. The Spirit himself equips us to compare our lives with the Biblical portrait of the Christian and the assurance we derive from the process contributes to that inner testimony of the Spirit.

Moreover, for those who lack the inner testimony, evidence of a changed life should go a long way towards removing their doubts. I knew a deeply religious man who had no real love for the Bible. But when he trusted in Christ, his desire to know the Scriptures knew no bounds. To suggest that such a change is not the work of God the Holy Spirit is to deny the obvious. Such changes bear eloquent testimony to the power of the gospel.

Without the Spirit's aid, we would not understand the Scriptures anyway. We would not even know about the Spirit's gift of assurance. Just as the men who wrote the Scriptures were verbally inspired by the Spirit (1 Cor. 2:13), so we who read them, understand and apply them by the same Spirit (1 Cor. 2:14).

The Spirit's inner testimony is also the Spirit's assurance that I am justified by faith. This is obvious once we realize that justifying faith is saving faith. All whom God justifies are his children forever. Nothing will be able to separate us from the love of God that is in Christ Jesus our Lord (Rom. 8:39). There is no reason at all why we should not be *fully* persuaded of these glorious truths.

The one who delivers the 'not guilty' verdict is the Judge of all. He does not communicate this verdict to us directly, as in a court of law. It would not be to our advantage if he did. The provision he has made for us to test ourselves is sufficient because justifying faith always shows itself in our inner experience. It transforms our convictions, our hopes and aspirations and our likes and dislikes.

Further evidence that we have justifying faith will be seen in a new awareness of eternal realities. The Spirit of God will move the believer away from his fascination with the things of this world and begin to fix his eyes on Jesus (Heb. 12:1-2). He will discover that his faith does indeed give substance to the things he now hopes for. The very thought of his glorious destiny will fill him with delight (1 Peter 1:3-9).

Odd as it may seem to those who are strangers to God's grace, genuine faith will also show itself in the believer's grief over his sins. Those who do not have justifying faith will not be too disturbed about such things. Indeed, we can be sure that the 'faith' of the man who never mourns over his transgressions is bogus (Ps. 51:3-4).

Yet, alongside this ongoing sorrow for sin, a new and deep love for God will develop. This love is not merely a sentimental feeling as is often supposed. It is a response of the whole being to God's inexpressible love for us, poured into the believer's heart by the Spirit (Rom. 5:5). It expresses itself in the love of righteousness (1 John 2:29), the love of God's word (Ps. 119:92,97), and love for God's people (1 John 5:1-2).

When we face the question as to whether we love God or not, as we are commanded to do, that passionate love for God's righteousness, God's word and God's people will be reliable indicators. By love for God's word, I do not mean a love for the Seventeenth Century English of the Authorized Version, or any other version for that matter. The love I speak about is rather like the keen interest a young man takes in the love letters from his absent sweetheart. He is eager to understand what she is saying because he loves her. When she is with him for good, he will have no further interest in her letters.

And on the day we see Jesus and are in his presence forever, we shall have no further use for the Scriptures. Until that day dawns, they are God's love letters to us. The person who has no interest in them cannot love God.

We must not think of this love for righteousness, truth and fellowship as three separate activities. If, say, I have three hobbies — I love writing, I love painting and I love gardening — I can only engage in one at a time. And my love for painting does not make me love gardening. Nor does my love for writing make me a good artist. But love for God's righteousness, God's Word and God's people cannot be separated in this way. It is impossible to love God's word without loving

God's righteousness, just as it is impossible to love God's righteousness without also loving God's people.

Those who insist that conduct is more important than creed, and practice more important than preaching, fail to see this. Like the horse and carriage, the two belong together. For the believer, correct creed produces correct conduct. Biblical preaching leads to biblical practice. If what I passionately believe is defective, my behaviour will also be defective.

For this reason, testing whether or not I am biblical in my faith is important. It comes under the heading of internal evidence, but the practical outcome, to which we shall turn in a moment, is obviously external. We need to be aware, however, that it is possible to be intellectually persuaded that the Bible is true without my behaviour being changed in any way. Intellectual persuasion without love is unproductive.

For many years now I have found it helpful to classify doctrines as primary or secondary. The question I pose to determine the issue is simple. If I deny this doctrine, or that, will it keep me out of the kingdom of heaven? If the answer is 'no', it is a secondary doctrine and, almost certainly, one about which Christians must agree to disagree. If 'yes', then it is a primary doctrine. I commend the practice to you.

If we are not persuaded about some secondary doctrine, it does not necessarily mean that we have failed the test. Sincere believers are always learning and should always be willing to upgrade their beliefs as Scripture provides more light. A closed mind on this matter is a serious handicap to growth. Proudly digging one's heels in on peripheral matters — a sin of which Christians are often guilty — is a hindrance both to growth and to fellowship.

Not least among the tests of our beliefs will be the question as to whether we joyfully acknowledge that Jesus is the long promised Messiah, Saviour of the world. 'If you do not believe that I am (the one I claim to be),' Jesus said to the Jews, 'you will indeed die in your sins' (John 8:24). The meaning is plain. Jesus claimed to be the great 'I AM'

(Exod. 3:14). He was saying: 'Unless you believe that I am God you will die in your sins'. If then, we do not wholeheartedly believe that Jesus is the Christ (Matt. 16:16), our 'faith' is useless. A similar statement occurs in John 3:36: 'Whoever believes in the Son has eternal life, but whoever rejects the Son will not see life, for God's wrath remains on him.'

External evidence

The Greek word *agape,* the word used for Christian love in the New Testament, is an action word. The question, therefore, that I need to ask myself is not 'Do I feel loving?' but 'How do I show my love for God and neighbour?' In particular, 'Do I have a special love for God's family?' According to Paul, love 'binds everything together in perfect harmony' (Col. 3:14). If we imagine all the fruits of the Spirit as bricks — joy, peace, patience, kindness, goodness, faithfulness, gentleness and self-control (Gal. 5:22), love must be seen as the mortar. To put it negatively, without love everything falls apart.

The test must not be restricted in its application. Liking my brother is not the same as loving my brother. Liking is natural, but loving is supernatural, especially when it comes to loving the unlovely. Of course, it is right for believers to have special friends — but, as Jesus said, 'If you love those who love you, what reward will you get? Are not even the tax collectors doing that?' (Matt. 5:46. In Jesus' time on earth, tax collectors were the undesirables.)

The apostle John's first letter fills out this test. 'We know that we have passed from death to life, because we love our brothers. Anyone who does not love remains in death. Anyone who hates his brother is a murderer, and you know that no murderer has eternal life in him' (1 John 3:14-15). The apostle is saying that hatred is like murder because the hater wants the hated to perish. No one who hates God's children will inherit eternal life. If we have no love for God's people and find the company of Christians irksome, we may safely assume our faith is counterfeit.

Finally, here's a test that will become more meaningful in later life for those who are now 'young in the faith'. It is the test of perseverance. In terms of priority, it would come near the top of the list, but usually a lot of water flows under the bridge before the importance of this test is appreciated. 'To the Jews who had believed him, Jesus said, "If you hold to my teaching, you are really my disciples. Then you will know the truth, and the truth will set you free"' (John 8:31-32).

The Lord Jesus was emphatic. Steady progress in the Christian life — holding to Christ's teaching — is vital evidence of the genuineness of our faith. We can be sure that those to whom God gives justifying faith will never fall away. Therefore, those who do not fall away have the evidence that they are justified. They are the ones who will grow in the knowledge of the truth and experience the glorious freedom it brings — freedom from the bondage of sin, from the condemnation of sin, from the guilt of sin and, largely, from the power of sin.

Much more could be said but there is enough here for the reader to determine where he stands. In all these things, there is the inevitable correspondence between his new experience and what the Scriptures teach. Although it becomes unhealthy to spend too much time in examining oneself, shortcuts are not to be recommended. Like a car, we cannot be on the road all the time. The vehicle needs regular inspection. But it is designed for service and is not much use if it is always in the garage, in bits. We too are called to serve, and we need to be at our best without spending too much time 'tinkering with the engine'.

Be honest with yourself

When some unbelievers face death, they have become so hardened that they have no thought of facing God's justice. Why not? They have become masters of the art of persuading themselves that heaven and hell are the stuff of fairy tales. It has become such a habit with them that, when lingering doubts arise about God and how they stand with him, they just switch off. It is impossible to conceive of a more wretched state. Why should anyone, through either ignorance or pride, deceive himself to his own hurt?

Others die, knowing that they have absolutely nothing to plead and rely completely on the mercy of God. They know that God has accepted them by faith as if they were righteous. They pass the test with flying colours and have that deep-seated assurance that to be 'away from the body' is to be 'at home with the Lord' (2 Cor. 5:8).

Writing to the Thessalonians, Paul graphically describes the judgement of those who reject Christ. The Lord Jesus will be 'revealed from heaven in blazing fire with his powerful angels. He will punish those who do not know God and do not obey the gospel of our Lord Jesus. They will be punished with everlasting destruction and shut out from the presence of the Lord and from the majesty of his power...' (2 Thess. 1:7-9). To the church in Rome, he says: 'For those who are self-seeking and who reject the truth and follow evil, there will be wrath and anger' (Rom. 2:8).

Finally, if, in spite of everything, you are still clinging to the hope that your good deeds will outweigh your bad ones, please remember that God requires perfect obedience to his commands. Good deeds cannot atone for bad ones. 'Whoever believes in him is not condemned, but whoever does not believe stands condemned already because he has not believed in the name of God's one and only Son' (John 3:18). 'What will you do on the day of reckoning, when disaster comes from afar? To whom will you run for help? Where will you leave your riches?' (Isa. 10:3).

So 'Examine yourselves to see whether you are in the faith; test yourselves. Do you not realize that Christ Jesus is in you — unless, of course, you fail the test?' (2 Cor. 13:5). This is not an examination like the ones you had in school or college. You had no way of knowing if you could answer the questions until you saw the exam paper. When it comes to examining ourselves in the matter of our faith, we are not disadvantaged in this way. The Scriptures supply the questions in advance.

Be careful not to miss your next medical check-up. If you do, problems you did not know about may cause some temporary inconvenience. Be even more careful not to miss your next spiritual check-up. Some sin, that may cause you to 'suffer loss' (1 Cor. 3:15), may remain uncovered.

Bildad, one of Job's would-be comforters, posed the question: 'How then can a man be righteous before God?' (Job 25:4). No one will ever be faced with a more important question. Centuries later, the apostle Paul provided the answer: 'A man is not justified by observing the law, but by faith in Jesus Christ' (Gal. 2:16). Knowing the answer in your head will not save you. You must know it in your heart as well.

Why I love Jesus

A personal testimony

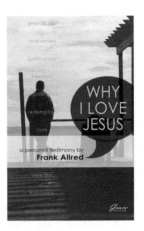

Here is a lively, intensely personal book; compact, yet full of scriptural truth. In 23 short chapters, Frank Allred explains in plain language why he loves Jesus – and why we should, too!

Why I love Jesus — a personal testimony, Frank Allred

ISBN: 9780946462735, Grace Publications

Fix your eyes on Jesus

In this his latest book Frank Allred urges us to fix our eyes upon Jesus. For the more we do so the more precious he will be to us and the more Christ-centred our lives will become.

In a day in which many Christians seem to go in for a quick fix spiritually, Frank Allred pleads with us to make every effort to become more aware of the glory of Christ and the privileges that are ours in him. We need also to realise afresh the glorious destiny that awaits us beyond this life — the enjoyment of God's new world in which there is neither sin nor death.

If we would know more of Christ (which is surely the desire of every true believer) we must immerse ourselves in the Bible for therein we shall find every reason to keep our eyes fixed on Jesus.

Fix your eyes on Jesus, Frank Allred

ISBN: 9780946462650, Grace Publications